From *INTEGRITY* Magazine

FATHER-HOOD

VOLUME 3

**Reclaiming
the Catholic
Head of the
Family for
Our Lord
Jesus Christ**

and FAMILY

VOLUME THREE

ANGELUS PRESS
2918 TRACY AVENUE, KANSAS CITY, M
(816) 753-3150 ♦ FAX (816) 7

The illustration used on the cover is a detail from a drawing which appeared on the cover of *Integrity*, vol.6, no.1, October 1951.

Library of Congress Cataloging-in-Publication Data

Fatherhood and the family.
      p. cm. – (From Integrity magazine : v. 3)
  ISBN 0-93-595229-2 (alk. paper)
   1. Fatherhood–Religious aspects–Catholic Church. 2. Thomas Aquinas, Saint, 1225?-1274. 3. Family–Religious life. I. Angelus Press. II. Series.
BX2352.5.F38 1999
261.B'358742–dc21   99-32721

ANGELUS PRESS
2918 TRACY AVENUE
KANSAS CITY, MISSOURI 64109
PHONE (816) 753-3150
FAX (816) 753-3557
ORDER LINE 1-800-966-7337

ISBN 0-935952-29-2
FIRST PRINTING—June 1999

Printed in the United States of America

CONTENTS

A MAN'S SOUL

A MAN'S FAMILY

A Man's Work and Wealth

The Man in Society

FOREWORD

This book is for men. Catholic men. For fathers and future fathers. The family is the first cornerstone of society and the key to the rebuilding of Christendom. Because it is men who start and father families, then fathers are the point-men in establishing society under Christ the King. Christendom starts here. Fathers are *the* essential first element of a constructive program for a Christ-centered Catholic America.

The minds of men must be convinced of this before men can want to do something about it. To help, we enlisted the assistance of our colleague, Fr. Thomas Scott, to assemble these essays from *INTEGRITY*, a radical Catholic magazine published from 1946-55. Do not be fooled: despite the fact that they are 50 years old, they are not "outdated." (*INTEGRITY* was way ahead of its time.) The principles they discuss are timeless. And while *INTEGRITY* never boasted of having the solutions to all the problems confronting Catholic men and their families, it certainly raised all the right questions. The essays have been kept pretty much intact as they first appeared.

In the *Contents* on the previous pages, we have classified the essays under four headings, building from the particular to the general. A man must know his Catholic manhood before he can bring its effects into his family and society. A man must be in league with Our Lord Jesus Christ before he can league his family with others to build a society of Our Lord Jesus Christ.

A one-line summary of each entry appears under each essay title in the *Contents* and a slightly longer one opens each essay throughout the book. Men, take the book into the bathroom with you and read what grabs you. To put it into practice, read the rest of it before the Blessed Sacrament.

A fatherless America is our nation's most urgent social problem, says David Blankenthorn (*Fatherless America*, 1995), and we agree. Over the past 200 years, American fathers have moved from the center to the fringe of family life. The Industrial Revolution and the modern economy have taken men out of their families and the vacuum has been filled by a steady feminization of the home. In the 1830's, Alexis de Tocqueville noted that the "influence of democracy" in America led to the fact that "paternal authority, if not destroyed, is at least impaired" (*Democracy in America*). Of this same period, Joseph Pleck comments: "[A] gradual and steady shift toward a greater role for the mother and a decreased and indirect role for the father, is clear and unmistakable" (*American Fathering in Historical Perspective*, 1987). Increasingly, men have looked outside the home for the meaning of their maleness. Masculinity has become less domesticated, defined less by effective fatherhood and more by individual ambition and achievement. But Catholic fatherhood is not simply bravado and bread-winning.

The role of fatherhood—*Catholic* fatherhood, we must add—has been diminished in three ways. First, it has become smaller. Fewer things are defined as a father's distinctive work. Secondly, fatherhood has been devalued. Today's public debate argues that fathers are simply not very important. Third, and most important, fatherhood has been decultured–stripped of any authoritative social content or definition (David Blankenthorn). In a Catholic context, a "decultured fatherhood" produces a "doubtful manhood" and castrates fathers from being the builders and preservers of Catholic culture. The connection between maleness and responsible Catholic fatherhood has disintegrated. "Being male is one thing," says Blankenthorn, "being a good father is another." To paraphrase Blankenthorn, without a return to the norms of effective Catholic fatherhood to anchor masculinity, the male project itself is doomed.

The question is, "What do fathers do?" The tragedy of our society is that it can't answer the question and neither can most Catholics.

This book is a stab at the Catholic answer.

If you are a lady buying this book, do not make a big deal of it to your husband and nag him to read it. If you do, he won't. Remember that you're not a man nor can you ever be a good father, despite your best intentions. To convince you of this, please read, "Holiness for Men," "The Family Has Lost Its Head," and "A Man's Work." You must cooperate with your husband, pray for him, but not replace him nor re-fashion him into your own image and likeness. To change a man, you don't visibly (in *his* sight) try to change him. Instead, admire and praise his good points (there must be some which were good enough for you to agree to marry him) and let the Holy Ghost do the rest. In other words, casually put the book on the coffee table, not on your husband's pillow with a condemnatory note and your order that he "Read, today!" If you do, you can be guaranteed he will make kitty litter of it. However, if you have a boy mature enough to handle the book, give it to him. Do so only with your suggestion that it will help him become a man. Do not make any derogatory comments or comparisons in relation to his father. You'll destroy your own credibility. (Remember, *you* married him.)

Men, when you have recognized the value of this book, be sure to take your son through it. Live it as you read it with him, however, or it'll be just another textbook to your boy.

> But do thou speak what befits the sound doctrine: that elderly men be reserved, honorable, prudent, sound in faith, in love, in patience;....Exhort the younger men, in like manner, to be self-controlled. Show thyself in all things an example

of good works, in teaching, in integrity and dignity; let thy speech be blameless, so that anyone opposing may be put to shame, having nothing bad to say of us (Titus 2:1,2,6-8).

The lies against the True Religion have discredited all religion and all truth, even truths of *nature*, upon which the truths of supernature are built. The lies against nature—specifically those against the masculine nature—have undermined manly convictions and effectively unmanned men. Louis-Edouard-Désiré Cardinal Pie (1815-80), inspiration to Pope Pius X, and known as the Bishop of Poitiers, a city-district of France, identified the problem over a hundred years ago:

> Is not ours an age of mislived lives, of unmanned men? Why?...Because Jesus Christ has disappeared. Wherever the people are true Christians, there are men to be found in large numbers, but everywhere and always, if Christianity wilts, men wilt. Look closely, they are no longer men but shadows of men. Thus what do you hear on all sides today? The world is dwindling away, for lack of men; the nations are perishing for scarcity of men, for the rareness of men....I do believe: there are no men where there is no character; there is no character where there are no principles, doctrines, stands taken; there are no stands taken, no doctrines, no principles, where there is no religious faith and consequently no religion of society. Do what you will: only from God will you get men [Homily on Christmas, 1871].

God give us a few good men.
St. Joseph, Pillar of Families, pray for them.
Men, your move.

Fr. Kenneth Novak
June 3, 1999
Feast of Corpus Christi

HOLINESS FOR MEN

Ed Willock

Masculine holiness is on trial. The Catholic religion is not just for women and children, but there are reasons why its practice has taken on an effeminate cast and why otherwise good men are justifiably turned off. The author cites four reasons how this situation has evolved in the Church and suggests a two-pronged first step to restoring masculine holiness which, in any case, must be lived if it is to endure.

By His own statement we are assured that Christ is less concerned about those who climb the tortuous paths of Mount Carmel than He is about the souls who wander directionless through the woods on the plains below. Many who are seeking God elsewhere than in His Church are not so much perverse in their choice of direction as misinformed by the false signposts erected by those who consider themselves among the elect. Among these wanderers are the men who have falsely concluded that "religion is for women and children."

Those who frequently have encountered this remark uttered with emphatic vehemence will recall that certain tonal inflections and gestures implied a heresy not explicate in the words themselves. The argument presented more accurately would be stated, "religion is for women and children *prima-*

rily" or "religion is for women and children *exclusively.*"

This attitude persists in varying degrees among many Catholic men today, much to the astonishment of the Church Militant, the Church Suffering and the Church Triumphant. Abraham and Moses, we can be sure, are not amused, nor is their brother patriarch of the New Testament, St. Patrick. The glorious choir of the apostles takes quiet but forceful difference with the contention of effeminacy. The admirable company of prophets shake their glorified beards in tangible evidence of masculinity. The white-robed army of martyrs, composed of both sexes, unhesitatingly testifies that religion merits the blood of men, whether male or female.

Those lesser saints, our venerable European forebears who fought manfully, lived verily and sometimes died courageously in the Faith so that we might inherit the gift, raise their baritone voices in protest at such a calumny. A clergy, masculine from cover to core, could not concur with such a view. If all that were not enough, the nail-pierced hands of Christ, calloused by years of manual labor, can be presented as clinching evidence of the masculinity of the Faith.

The temptation after such testimony is to throw the case out of court. On the surface the charge of effeminacy seems rash and unsubstantiated. We should, however, give the plaintiff an opportunity to state his case. In answer to the foregoing defense of the masculine nature of piety, his rebuttal might go like this: "You have proved only that Christianity is originally and traditionally masculine. If it is a living Faith, what evidence have we here in America that religion evokes a masculine piety or provokes a masculine dynamism? Show me signs of a virile Faith among American Catholic men!"

This question cannot be answered glibly. It cannot be pushed aside as irrelevant. We may recall the news stories of priests in war and peace administering with heroic courage

to the needs of souls. Processions of Holy Name men and
other public manifestations of masculine piety can be produced as evidence. But are these enough? Are they typical or
isolated events? What about the vast majority of Catholic
laymen? Can we point to their way of life as examples of
Christian idealism and aspiration in startling contrast to their
non-Catholic friends? I think not. I think masculine piety is
on trial, and we might well examine the situation and make
some sort of judgment.

One fact that is quite obvious is that religion appeals to
the man in a different way from the way it appeals to the
woman. It is the same Faith, it evokes the same virtue, but
the disposition to it is different. As religious experience ma-
tures, as it passes from the elementary stage of psychological
and intellectual union to sanctity and mystical union, the
appeal and response tend to become the same regardless of
sex. Until spiritual maturity is achieved, however, the psychology of the sexes is an important instrument in conversion and growth.

When stating a proposition concerning the psychological peculiarities of the sexes, a writer runs the risk of all sorts
of misunderstandings. To avoid this as much as possible please
bear in mind these qualifications of what I have to say. Psychology deals with tendencies, not qualities. The masculine
and feminine persons represent two essential possibilities of
the *same nature.* They are both equal in potentialities and
equal in dignity. It is because they are essentially incomplete
and oriented to each other that they tend to follow parallel
and converging paths rather than identical paths. Neither
revelation nor common sense admits of any essential inferiority of one sex to the other. The gifts are of equal value.
The dependence is mutual. When I use the word *effeminate*
I use it in a derogatory sense as distinct from the word *femi-*

nine. Effeminacy is a softness, a lack of discipline, a sensate romanticism which is a despicable characteristic either in man or woman. It is a perversion of feminine virtue just as ruthlessness and rationalism are a perversion of masculine virtue.

Human behavior shows that the tendency in the woman is to be concerned with persons and particulars. The tendency in the man is to be concerned with things and generalities. The loyalty of the woman usually finds its object in a responsive person. The loyalty of the man usually finds its object in a compelling cause. These facts, I believe are self evident and, fortunately, they are the only facts I need for the development of my argument.

Religion is loyalty to a God Who can be conceived of as a Person (for He is a Person) or a Cause (for He is *the* Good).

The saints know God as He is in Himself, as both the Person Who loves and is loved and as the Cause to be pursued and attained. In the first stages of holiness, however, the woman tends to seek a personal relationship of love whereas the man tends to seek a moving and satisfying ideal.

Now there is something paradoxical in the two conceptions of God, one as a Person and the other as an Ideal. As human beings we find it difficult to separate the idea of a person from the idea of a particular individual. For us, the idea of a person excludes all other persons. On the other hand the concept of an ideal abhors particularization. Goodness, justice, liberty, or love, are nothing unless they are universal and non-exclusive.

Since the Person with whom she seeks communion is invisible, the particular tangible instruments of the Faith become the loving object of the woman's devotion. Since the Ideal to which he aspires is a universal, the man is loath to limit this ideal to any particular place, form, or priesthood.

Until the paradox of particularity and catholicity is resolved, the man is disturbed by the very limitations which appeal to the woman. She loves the church and the priest, the altar and the rosary, the hymn and the formal prayer because they are so familiar, so close and so tangible. He is suspicious of these things because they are so localized, so exclusive and familiar that they hardly seem to do justice to the Ideal which is all-inclusive, all-embracing.

At any time in history or in any place on the globe, this divergence of attitude between man and woman can be expected. In our time and in this country, the situation has been aggravated by the fact that practical Catholicism has assumed an effeminate cast. This effeminacy, evidenced in liturgical practices and standards of conduct, with emphasis on the personal, the sensate, the devotional, cannot be attributed to any one cause but to a number of historical trends both within and without the Church. These trends can be categorized loosely under the heading of secularism, and secularism has resulted in:

(1) The relegation of religion to one phase of human activity.

(2) The confinement of religion to the area of the church and the school.

(3) The regarding of the religious act as a personal secret quite divorced from any vital social significance.

(4) The divorce of faith from reason as though they were irreconcilable.

It is obvious that religion telescoped to such narrow dimensions focuses undue emphasis upon the aspects of the Faith most appealing to the feminine psychology. The home, the church and the school become for the Catholic mother the angles of a familiar triangle. She tends to direct her religious perceptions almost exclusively to that enclosure. These are her daily and particular concern because they involve the children and are within the scope of her normal interests. Man's activities and interests, even though they may radiate from the home, find their target in the shop and office, and the social and political problems of the day. All of these places and problems have been long divorced from religion as to ends as well as means. Whenever he enters the religious sphere, the man feels that he is in some sense entering the domain of the woman. Any parochial activity not specifically for men is, *per se*, for women. The Ideal, that concept of God psychologically attractive to man, can only touch him when it is made manifest in the work world, professional world, scientific world, and political world with which he is in contact. The secularist divorce which sets the mystical against the practical, and the facts of revelation against the facts of sensible observation, by inference pushes religion over to the distaff side of the table. This localization of religion to the secret intercourse and the parish buildings has produced the ghetto-Catholicism very apparent in many quarters. It would not be hard to prove that the ghetto complex is basically effeminate even when it expresses itself in violently defensive apologetics. The Ideal is catholic and of cosmic scope; it is affirmative and universal, impatient of ghettos, desirous of assimilating all things, assured of its universality. The spiritually immature man can be sympathized with when he is disheartened by a restricted, particularized, sensate, localized and maternal religiosity so at variance with the Ideal to which he clumsily aspires. The sight of such a facade is enough to drive him away before he has time to enter and discover that there is less contradiction in localized Catholicism than he first supposed. The fact that the Faith is being sold short tends to make the prospect underestimate its true value.

Few active Catholics are unaware of the general irresponsibility of men toward their religious duties. Steps have already been taken to restore liturgical practices to their proper purity which would remove the effeminacy and make them more psychologically appealing to men. Priests everywhere are working to induce men to come closer to the altar. Religion teachers of boys and young men are striving to masculinize religion. We are indebted to them (perhaps as much for their errors as for their successes) for making it possible to make certain suggestions for improvement tested by practice.

The great danger, I think, is that a study of the tendencies peculiar to man and woman might lead us to use such studies as a norm for prescribing apostolic techniques. We can make the mistake of supposing that that which is most psychologically attractive is the best form to use. That is too much like asking a patient to prescribe his own medicine. More than that it excludes, or merely tolerates, all of the unpleasant things that no one likes, such as sacrifice, suffering, penance and contrition.

An example of the false principle in practice would be to have parochial fashion shows for women who are already jeopardizing their souls' salvation by an inordinate interest in clothes. Another is parochial emphasis on sports for men who are already neglecting their Christian and patriotic responsibilities in pursuit of sports. Even in the hierarchy of psychological urges there is usually something higher to appeal to than vanity and playfulness. The lady parishioner who puts on the latest creation is less disposed if anything to put on her Creator. The virility of sports is not so contagious that religion will get it by contact. I realize that these things are merely "come-ons" to attract the people and are usually quite distasteful to the priest who uses the technique. It is

my experience that such methods actually repel the people
who would go to get pure and unadulterated religious training. If religion does not attract people in a day when people
are hungry for a faith, it is not because religion is lacking in
secular glamor but because religion is being spiked with adul-
terating syrups.

If the male or female psychology does not prescribe the
technique of appeal, then of what use is the inquiry into the
peculiarities of each? The answer is simply that Catholicism
lived (not doctrine, nor a technique, nor a movement, nor a
view), a living presence in a person, in a family, in a community, has an appeal to both men and women equally. Men
may dislike devotional services, women may dislike study
clubs, but they both like supernatural charity. Men may dislike sugary hymns and women may dislike sermons on union-
ism, but they both like supernatural fortitude. We need not
look further for proof of this than the Catholic Worker
movement. Whatever else the Catholic Worker has done, it
has given an example of supernatural charity and supernatural fortitude that has attracted the interest of thousands. Literally hundreds of men have sought out the Catholic Worker
houses because full-blooded, unadulterated virtue has an
appeal that cannot be ignored. Even those who differ with
the Catholic Worker opinions in whole or in part cannot
deny the heroic virtue evidenced in its leaders.

If religion does not appeal to men, an inquiry into the
reasons can help us, not by showing how to *present* the Faith,
but how to practice it. The Faith when lived generates its
own form. When it is lived it may provoke love and it may
provoke hate, but never indifference.

Why is it that many men do not see the Ideal in Catholic
life? I think it is because we Catholics do not exhibit either
austerity or catholicity. The story is told of the man who

sold all that he had to purchase the jewel of great price. This is the sort of testimony lacking today. As far as the outsider can see, the price of the jewel of Faith is adherence to a group of precepts in theory if not in practice, the obligation of Sunday Mass and a meatless diet on Fridays. The same Catholic in pursuit of a better standard of living exhibits a much greater propensity for sacrifice than he does in pursuit of the Ideal. The state also sets a higher price on citizenship through the levying of taxes, the ordering of our lives, and the asking of the same life in time of war. In the open market, for everyone to see, the jewel of Faith is marked down to a price lower than that of loyalty to mammon and loyalty to the state. It is difficult for the uninitiated to see that the jewel is worth more than the price quoted.

The key to the problem of masculine piety, to my mind, is found in the word *Catholic*. The word Catholic as an adjective to describe the Faith has a vertical as well as a horizontal meaning. The horizontal meaning is that, as a way of supernatural life, Christianity is for all mankind, and that the fruits of the Incarnation and the doctrine of salvation are meant for all men at all times. The Church was instituted to spread the Faith across the globe and down the centuries, alive in substance, precise in doctrine, healing and uplifting in its effect. The vertical meaning is that the nature of the Faith is to reorient all men and all things to God. There is nothing to which the Faith is irrelevant, and the relevance of everything is found in the Faith.

This vertical aspect of the Faith is seldom revealed in the attitudes and habits of today's Catholics. When it is understood and acted upon, men will see clearly that Catholicism is the ideal. They will see that Catholicism demands that Christ be the center and orientation of all our acts and all our desires. The jobs that we hold, the vocations we choose, the studies we pursue, the companions we keep, the recreation we enjoy, the ambitions to which we aspire, only make Christian sense if they are orientated to God and this not merely by intention but by their nature and end.

To summarize, we can say that men fail to see in Catholicism as generally practiced the all-embracing Ideal which is their first immature concept of God. They fail to see it first, of course, because of their spiritual immaturity, but also because the Faith as generally practiced has become effeminate and localized. We cannot very well increase their maturity until we have first attracted them to the spiritual director and the Sacraments. So the first step must be a testimony to them of austerity (as against effeminacy) and catholicity (as against localization).

It must be understood that in this particular case we cannot let the patient prescribe his own medicine. In other words, we are not looking for tricks and tactics artificially devised with which to lure the men into the churches. If men currently find juke boxes, beer, and sports inordinately appealing, that has nothing to do with us. From us they want some evidence of the Ideal, an ideal which when acquired will give them a joy, a stimulation and a virility that they are seeking now in the juke boxes, beer and sports.

Catholicism Lived

Stated in the fewest possible words the thing they seek, whether they know it or not, is an evidence of Catholicism *lived*. Catholicism lived is austere and it is catholic, and it is the only convincing testimony that Catholicism is directed to the Ideal.

Catholicism lived sounds very much like a definition of sanctity, but sanctity is not precisely what I mean. Catholicism lived is a group manifestation of Christian virtue, organized on the social level, unified on the intellectual level and orientated to God on the spiritual level. Just as the saint, as an isolated phenomenon, demonstrates the orientation of human personality to God, Catholicism lived is a community of persons which demonstrates the orientation of human society to God. The aspiration to personal sanctity is implied in it and is the vitalizing factor, but it is the group testimony of integrated Catholic living which is the immediate end of such an organization.

Let's consider briefly the practical steps that might be taken to bring such a group into existence within a parish. The Holy Ghost will provide different counsels, different opportunities and different apostolic material in different areas. I only devise this set of practical suggestions in order to demonstrate more clearly the theory of Catholicism lived.

Suppose we choose as the conceptual day for this revolutionary parochial venture the Feast of Christ the King, October 31. This great feast upon which day the Church makes present the coronation of Christ, King of all mankind, the end of all free and necessary activity in the universe, seat of benevolence and judgment, the proper object of all men's desires, works and prayers, is the most appropriate day for instituting a new order founded in Christ. The coming of the King should be anticipated with the same vigor and widespread proclamation as is usually occasioned by the annual parochial bazaar. Cards, posters, tickets, flyers, announcements, should be drawn up in bold and colorful phrases, telling of the advent of King Christ to reign over the entire world and specifically over that parish. Special emphasis should be brought to bear on the men of the parish, especially those who have been bored or dismayed by the dull complacency of the old era which is about to die. Mothers, wives and girl friends should be encouraged to impress upon

their men that a new era of masculine piety is about to begin. Every man should be urged to go to Confession and
Communion, leaving as little loophole for excuse as they get
on Mother's Day.

The Day of the King will begin with a High Mass at
6:00am (Perhaps a vigil service the night before will get the
men to bed early so that they can get up for this early Mass.)
At the High Mass a sermon will be preached on Christ the
King, Lord of our souls, Lord of our lives, Lord of our country, Lord of the universe, *etc.* Emphasis will be on austerity
in His cause and catholicity in its furtherance.

The same sermon will be preached at all other Masses
with the inference that all those who do not participate in
the celebration of the feast are nothing less than traitors. In
the afternoon there will be vespers, benediction and a procession, rain or shine (preferably rain so that everyone will
get soaking wet). The procession will be to crown a statue of
Our Lord, King of the Universe. The men will march at-
tired in their work clothes, each carrying a tool of his trade
or an object of his craft. Working girls will do the same.
These objects will be blessed and offered as symbols of the
sacrifice of the man in his work to Christ. Each family, in
the person of the husband, will be annexed to the new-found
kingdom. Every child should be present to see his father and
mother joined together in their new dedication.

After the procession a banquet will be served with food
prepared by the housewives. It will be informal, noisy, friendly
(no stuffed shirts or professional waiters). The less organized
preparation for the banquet the better it will be. What one
housewife lacks another will provide. Men and women will
get to know their neighbors, exchanging a sandwich for an
apple, or a bottle opener for a shaker of salt.

In the evening the baby-sitting teenagers will take over

the children while the mothers and fathers, and the single men and single women, attend the first council of the government of Christ the King. The object of this meeting will be to get men and women to be the lay leaders of Catholic Action groups in the parish (for Catholic Action is the structure of the new kingdom). The qualifications for leadership must be rigorous: daily Mass and Communion, completely dedicated lives, apostolicity in society, the firm resolution to integrate their daily lives with the Faith.

These leaders when enrolled will be the contact of the laity with the priest. Working with their neighbors, they will carry the Faith out into those areas from which the priest has been excluded. He will mold their spirituality, bringing their immature zeal to a full fruition.

An inquiry conducted on various nights throughout the octave will help the leaders determine what practical problems they must focus their attention upon. The hidden kingdom of Christ in the heart must be made incarnate and visible through some particular apostolate. Perhaps a family apostolate will be the suggestion, or the Christianization of the local factory, or a missionary activity to help the Negro. The local need will stipulate the proper action to be taken.

When these organizations hit their stride the man who says "religion is for women and children" will have to do so in secret. The austerity of Catholicism lived, of families accepting their due quota of children as new subjects of Christ the King, of charity so that there is no one in need within the parish whether Catholic or not, of social justice unrelaxed in its vigilance to see that everyone receives his due, of catholicity in contributions of money and goods wherever in the world the need may be, of inquiry-searching the mind of God for new evidence of His greatness, and searching the universe for new fields to be redeemed, is that kind of austerity that will be masculine and Catholic beyond words.

When the newcomer enters the climate generated by a Catholicism lived, the paradox that bothered him will be resolved. The Good which he sought will soon be recognized as a personal, intimate God, localized in the Eucharist but yet Lord of the universe, particularized in His Church yet the proper object of the adoration of every nation.

The mature participation of the men by the same token will enlarge the field of the women's religious perceptions. They will recognize *my* God as *the Good.* They will see the direct relationship between social justice in unions, for the Negro, for the Jew, for the poor, and the *my* God of their spiritual devotion. The beholder will see in the activity of men and women living the Faith the reconciliation of the paradox of a God Who is the familiar object of devotion and *the Good* under Whose banner armies of men will march forever.

THE CONFIRMED HERO

Ed Willock

The whole phenomenon of hero-worship is peculiar. The adulation of sports, movie, and rock stars trains us to think that heroes are more-than-human. The heroics of holiness, however, deals precisely with very human and very everyday things. At the same time, however, sanctity has a breathtaking disregard for the world's standards. Catholicism *lived* is risky, daring, and heroic.

I can think of nothing that so pointedly indicates the need for a revival of risk and adventure in modern living than the thing we pedantically refer to as juvenile delinquency. We should be more honest and more accurate to call it youthful frustration. If it were true that there was no apparent reason for frustration, then we could treat the malady as something vicious and personal. If modern living offered every adventurous opportunity that a youthful heart desires, then hot-rod escapades, armed assault, dope addiction and the like, are evidence of a kind of mass-mania quite beyond explaining.

This is not the case. If we were more sympathetic with our teenagers, we should see through their more innocent eyes the most alarming weakness in modern society. It would be as apparent to us as it is to them that an era of Ease,

Comfort, and Protection (industrial society's sole reason for being) is at the same time infernally dull. To have capitulated to such bovine temptations as these is a sign of a great sickness, a sickness which our teenagers wisely prefer not to contract. It is the mark of our social degradation if the only two alternatives presented to our youth for daring-do are hot-rods and air-foam mattresses. The young man who prefers to drive madly through the night in a souped-up heap rather than be a nice boy and make lots of money at a "respectable" job has alas (we should admit it) chosen the better part.

The thing about Catholicism that has always had a great appeal to youth is the breathtaking disregard it has for worldly standards. In the midst of men who stand clinging to their possessions, jealous of their lusts, fearful for their carcasses, the Christian walks cheerfully, freely, and defiantly. Is this the tradition that we have permitted to shine through our lives? Is it the Catholic father who tells his son: "Use your talents for Christ; you won't make much money and people will laugh at your idealism, but you will find adventure in a great cause!" Or is it more likely that he will drag in religion on a string in order to bolster a purely worldly set of standards: "You have a moral obligation to make a good living. Catholicism doesn't expect heroism!"

No Risk, No Daring

The Catholic parent or teacher may know every possible argument to justify astute ambition, ambiguous diplomacy. He may know twenty arguments against the rashness of "working for nothing," "starry-eyed idealism," having a lot of kids, mixing religion with politics, dirty poverty, yet in winning the argument he will be unable to eradicate the suspicion from his son's mind that he and his ilk have sold Christianity down the river in exchange for protection, pills, and pensions. Only a very sick mind could fall for the modern "bargain" by which one gives up all idealism, Christian or human, for the sake of preserving one's safety, one's income, one's social standing. Are our children rabbits that we should expect them to desire nothing more sublime than food, clothing and shelter? Can we expect them to countenance our deceit that thousands of our predecessors have suffered persecution and death for a faith which we are willing to constrain so that it may fit into a scheme of avarice? Do we want them, as we have done, to become deceptively proficient in the service of two masters?

Granted that our youth, not necessarily through virtue but through instinct, reject the goal of fetal security to which we have dedicated our every daily talent. Are they wholly in the wrong when they indulge in madcap risks, if we have not borne witness to the fact that Catholicism is a militant, difficult and daring denial of all the conventions by which worldlings live? Let's ask ourselves pointedly, right now, whether Catholicism *lived* requires action which current criteria considers idealistic, rash, risky and "imprudent"?

Melodrama

We find ourselves in a strange sort of muddle today when we talk about heroism. The literature of the last generation spent most of its time debunking heroism, thus preparing the way for the popular acceptance of safety and security as a dignified mode of existence. Certain dramatic terms that once brought chills to the spines of our forebears—"Save the Old Homestead." "My Mother was a Lady!" "I'd rather die than say 'Yes.'" "Keep the Faith!"—are now occasions for hilarity. How naive to our more enlightened minds these corny heroics of ancient melodramas! Yet Catholics must blush

when they hear read moral directives which are just as "corny"
currently being preached from our pulpits. "Keep the faith!"
may be a jocular remark exchanged between bar-flies as they
stagger home to bed, but it is still the admonition St. Paul
addressed to his persecuted brethren.

It should be easy for thousands of Catholics to recall the
catechism definition of Confirmation which states that this
Sacrament gives us the grace and the responsibility "to profess our faith and rather die than deny it." Is this corn or is it
the thing Catholic men live by? We can't have it both ways.
This secular propaganda against heroic decision ridicules
every Christian virtue; the honest man is called a "sucker,"
the chaste girl is called a "prude," the generous mother of
children is called a "breeder," the man who wants to earn a
living by hard work rather than become a con-man is a "nature boy," the person anxious to give his life for anything
other than money is a "fool" or a "romantic." In my experiences these scathing names are just as likely to come from
Catholics as from anyone else.

Hero-Worshippers All

On the other hand, contradictorily enough, as a people
we are manufacturing heroes at a rate never before attempted.
Any person so innocent as to believe what he reads, after
scanning the daily sport-page must conclude that yesterdays
Dodger game outrivalled the battle of Lepanto in gore, glory
and gumption. The public is encouraged to gripe every time
the men who mine their coal ask for another dime-per-hour,
yet the heroes of Hollywood and Yankee Stadium are show-
ered with a king's ransom to spend as affluently as they please.

Ever since the Reformation the incidence of immortal-
ity among humans has been on the increase. The Church
canonizes some few dead saints every year; the daily press

canonizes a few living heroes every day. This adulation of ball-chasers, groaners, hams and "geniuses" educates us to the erroneous opinion that heroes are of a more-than-human species. Secular heroism revolves around the sensational, the bizarre, and the anarchic. These comic-strip attitudes toward heroes and heroism seriously contradict notions that are basic to Christianity. For example, Christianity teaches that a perfectability has been made attainable to *all men* as a result of Christ's becoming our Brother and dying for us, and it teaches further that *all men* are obliged to strive for this perfection. The only hero is the saint. Even here our half-secular, half-Catholic minds become confused. Suddenly the saint becomes another Frankie who takes to religion instead of to crooning!

It is only after a great deal of thoughtful effort that certain distinctions become clear. The kind of heroism demanded by Christianity is universal (attainable by every man) and contemporary (common to every age). Secular heroism is not divine election but human adulation, and thus marked for a special few and marked by a shifting of standards. St. Paul is a contemporary and universal figure, whereas yesterday's secular hero is tomorrow's stumble-bum.

If we confuse Christian heroism with secular heroism, we endow sainthood with certain romantic, exotic and bizarre features as an excuse for feeling no urge to let its appeal disrupt the bourgeois tenor of our own affairs. Yet the heroics of sanctity deal with commonplace things. Christ, Our Hero and Our Lord (leader), exemplified heroism in regard to commonplace matters. He suffered indigence, ingratitude, suffering and death. These, though somewhat less in intensity, are the common lot of every man. Saintly heroics are seldom a matter of going into the ring with Joe Louis, standing before a firing squad, hitting a home run at the Polo

Grounds, carrying a serum into the infected wilds of Tibet.
Usually sanctity deals with child-bearing, earning an honest
living, suffering pain, bearing ingratitude—all of them as
common to one side of the globe as to the other.

Refusing Common Sanctity

Yet how appropriate is this lesson to the modern world!
Are not the universal refusals of difficulties in our day primarily refusals—to bear children, to work honestly, to suffer
pain, to risk ingratitude? The common man is refusing the
common sanctity of Christianity. He is implying that heroism is the romantic behavior of special people—using this as
an excuse for supineness, timidity and luxury in his own
affairs.

A fastidious avoidance of risk and discomfort is a kind of
childishness; the child is accustomed to other people shoul-
dering risks and discomforts for him. It is highly significant
that during these days when a childish flight from difficulties has become epidemic among adults, the Christian Sacrament precisely created to stimulate maturity is looked upon
as a silly little ceremony of beribboned cuteness. The Sacrament designed to make us mature soldiers of Christ, giving
us the determination and confidence to bear an adult burden, has all the appearances of grown-up mammas playing
with their little dolls. The sign remains but its significance is
generally forgotten.

The Confirmed Christian

Confirmation, Christian adulthood, is the root from
which the dual shoots of Matrimony and Holy Orders grow.
A serious consciousness of adult vocation depends upon a
wholehearted co-operation with the graces of Confirmation.
If one could not see the results, one would still expect that

an ignorance of Confirmation would be followed by a refusal to take adult responsibility as an apostolic Catholic.

I shall not attempt here to go into any exhaustive treatment of this great Sacrament, but I should like to deal with a few self-evident truths which follow from its simple catechism definition. The traditional analogy is that of being enlisted in an army. The pat on the cheek administered by the bishop is the imparting of a divine commission. This road of Christian maturity is difficult, we are assured, but we travel it, not alone, but in a great company.

The Lone Sentry

One of its several effects is to urge us to confirm one another in the Faith. How scandalous it is if any confirmed Catholic is left to suffer alone! Where is the grand army of which he is part?—yet this loneliness has become far too typical. If a workman urged on by the virtue of justice attempts to organize a union among his fellows, is he likely to find himself surrounded by other confirmed Catholics who will see him through the trials that accompany such determination? Hardly! More than likely he is cautioned, "Take care of number one....Don't stick your neck out....Feather your own nest." When the mother of many children finds herself in a maternity ward, happy with her new baby and anxious to get home to the others, do other confirmed Catholic people surround her rejoicing in her triumph, encouraging her to face the new hardships? Hardly! More than likely if she is noticed at all it is to impart some warning, "How awful! Six children! You poor thing Don't you think you've done your share?"

If a young girl decides to attach herself to some Catholic activity which requires a lot of work and little reward, do her Catholic friends jump in and say, "It's a grand thing you're doing, stay with it." Hardly! She hears instead, "You're throwing your life away! You'll get no thanks....After all, what's in it for you!"

That's the way the story usually goes. Not only is the intrepid soul who follows his conscience against convention left to himself, but he is actually discouraged by those who claim to be in the same army as he! It is no wonder at all that widely-scattered Catholics from all walks of life write to each other like so many intimates, even though they may never have met, simply because they see in one another buddies in the same confirmed army. But these are the few. Where will you find a neighborhood so animated with Christian convictions? Why must the brethren be scattered?

When the early martyrs stepped into the dreadful arena, they did not see a group of their fellow Christians sitting in the front row, but they would today. Catholic living has become doubly difficult because it is attended by such utter loneliness. This could be excused if the typical interpretation by the zealous ones was to parade in sackcloth and ashes, or set up hermitages in the north woods. No, such simple things as having a fourth or fifth baby, or speaking out against flagrant injustice—in other words, just avoiding sin is now regarded as rashness. Timidity, luxury and barrenness have not grown spontaneously among our Catholic people; they have encouraged one another in it.

It has been my personal good fortune to encounter circumstances other than those I am describing here. My great blessing has been to have my faith constantly re-confirmed by the admirable actions of Catholic associates. Thus, when I make the above charges I do so without rancor, but insist that the laxity of most Catholics in this regard is common knowledge.

Fruit of the Community

It is time we admitted that there are far more enemies of Christianity in the world than atheistic Communism. It should not come as a surprise to us that individualism (one of our household gods) is *no less an enemy.* The inference that nobility of character occurs among humans with the same unpredictable individuation as epilepsy or double-jointedness is a subtle attack against the Catholic community—its very reason for existence is to create a spiritual climate in which human perfections become commonplace. The responsibility to be virtuous is a shared responsibility. Although an individual may from time to time grow in perfection *in spite of* the viciousness or weakness of his intimate associates, this should not be the rule. In the majority of cases in which Christian heroism is practiced, it comes not so much as a consequence of one man pitting himself against the world, but as a result of a well-defined community effort. The Christian hero is not a flash of glory, fire worked against nocturnal void: he is but one fruit upon a vast tree, a tree planted, pruned, enlivened for the sole purpose of generating heroic fruit. The Mass, the parish, the common effort of religious, virgins, and parents is a divinely organized attack upon fallen human nature. The heroic cancer patient manifests a greatness which is fruit of the combined efforts of her priest and brethren acting as a body under the Headship of Christ. The same is true of the overburdened parent, the honest workman, and all our other confirmed heroes.

The Protestant concept of holiness—a direct pipeline from individual to God unmodified by any mediatorship of Christ, Pope, priest, or community of saints—has lent credence to the secular notion of individualistic, self-generating heroism. In this false light human greatness appears to be an uncaused cause, rather than what it is—the expected effect of a divine-human organization designed to produce such results. When a Catholic acts in a fashion that appears to be heroic, more often than not he does so from the conviction that to do less would constitute a betrayal of the Faith. Likewise, when a Catholic fails to respond to what in his conscience appears to be an obligation on the premise that "Christianity does not require heroism," he is not merely refusing the invitation to be a hero, he is betraying the Faith. Too many people reject poverty, insecurity, sacrifice, loneliness and hard work as though these were special duties for heroic volunteers, neglecting the obvious fact that in particular instances the only alternative to these difficulties may be sin. For example, all the propaganda today in defense of non-conception of children is seldom an argument for heroic continence but a defense of sin. Yet the birth-controllers put up a common front with those who plead for continence and come up with a remarkable combination of the two called "Rhythm"! Another example is that of the wage-earner who hides behind his family as a reason for not sticking his neck out against a social injustice. Although many families may be ruined due to his unwillingness to face a difficult obligation, he excuses this on the basis that he is a God-fearing family man.

The Result of Timidity

Confirmation, then, a part of Christian living, makes every Catholic a special kind of hero and member of an heroic Body. If Catholics adopt the mentality of their times, they will excuse themselves from taking their share of the heroic burden, preferring to look upon the few who accept the burden as special people. Thus it appears as though "apostolic" Catholics are the queer ones who prefer to be queer, and that those who are timid and cautious in keeping with the secular mores are normal. The net result is to rob the zealous Catholic of the community support he has every reason to expect, and to place him in a position where to perform the simple duties of his state requires an heroic effort.

WHAT IS A GROWN-UP?

Ed Willock

The mature man is a custodian over life. Maturity is a state of reproductivity in at least four areas: parenthood, thought, art, and apostleship. Married men who reject their duty to father children and get them to heaven render life sterile in all these aspects. The mature custodian of life himself lives a life of self-sacrifice and mortification. Men will be immature and barren until they are connected with Christ.

It is an interesting fact, though not necessarily edifying, that the only people who can really insult one another in this day and age are Catholics. The modern mind which dilutes its wine with barley water and files the edge off every sharp instrument, has replaced the barb on the end of the insult with a soft rubber vacuum cup. Take for instance the adjective *immature*. This seems to be the best the modern can evoke in the way of an insult. Yet how weak an insult it is! First of all it doesn't sound like an insult. No polysyllabic word can be uttered with much vehemence, especially if it ends with *ure*. Just imagine (to prove my point) two truck drivers in traffic, with one calling the other immature! It is far too lady-like an insult to suit a virile circumstance.

More important than the sound of the word is the clammy psychological inference that usually goes with it which implies that the immature person is less guilty than sick. Immaturity, the modern implies, is something you catch like a cold. The insult becomes a soft baby-slap. "The poor dear doesn't know any better."

A Christian insult is a veiled compliment, that is to say, it is an admonition. It implies that whatever is wrong with you spiritually is to some extent your fault, and that you can correct it with God's help, which is always available for the asking. Certainly there is far more hopefulness in the diagnosis of ill-will than in the diagnosis of sickness. It is more of a compliment to say you are responsible, even for your irresponsibility, than to say that you are the sad prey of uncontrollable circumstances.

I consider this point a necessary introduction to a study of the chronic childishness and prolonged adolescence which is a sign of the times. You and I have a personal and social guilt in relation to the condition of adult irresponsibility. Simply because immaturity lacks the sharp edge of malice or brutality we are inclined to laugh it off as just good old human nature. We forget that immaturity and malice frequently have the same dire results, both here and hereafter.

The first step in the program is to define maturity. What does it mean to be grown up?

A Custodian of Life

We say a tomato plant is mature when it produces tomatoes. By the same token we can say a human being is mature when he marries another human being and has babies. This provides a factor in our definition, but it isn't wholly satisfactory. Having children is a sign of biological maturity; but man is not merely a biological being—this is a weakness in the comparison with the tomato plant. There is, however, a strong point in the comparison if we see in the two acts a discharge of an obligation owed to the species by the individual. The tomato plant is mature when it reproduces the life of the species. Man is mature when he reproduces the life of mankind. In childhood the individual gratuitously receives life and sustenance for its physical and spiritual growth. Justice would see in this the accumulation of a debt. The indebtedness is to mankind in general, to the parent and friend in particular, but the discharge of the debt lies not so much in the quarter from which the gift is received, but toward the new lives to be produced and sustained. When the individual takes up this responsibility and begins to discharge it, he is mature. The mature man is a custodian over life.

Four Kinds of Reproductivity

At first it might seem to be an over-simplification of maturity to equate it with parenthood. To say that maturity is a state of reproductivity is less a definition than a key that will open the door to a broader vista of the subject. There are other forms of human productivity besides parenthood. We could, for purposes of brevity, reduce the number to four.

Man reproduces life in four ways, through parenthood, through thought, through art and through apostolicity. Parenthood is a form of reproductivity that is pretty obvious. It is all very tangible and matter of fact. Thought and art are two categories that have become vague and romantic, encrusted with all sorts of silly notions. So let's talk about them.

Thinking, it can be presumed, is the natural function of any man who has a mind. The product of thought is an idea. When a mind has an idea, spirit produces spirit. There is a sort of wedding between the knowledge that man has and the things he observes, and out of this wedding a new life is

born, called an idea. Ideas, like children, must be nurtured
to maturity. To have an idea is both an occasion for rejoicing
and the beginning of responsibility. The realization, for example, that "God is good," implies the tremendous obligation of worship. To evolve the idea that "human freedom is
precious" may involve the responsibility of giving your life
to prove it. To conclude that "every man has a mission to
fulfill" is less a conclusion than a beginning. To think habitually "just for fun" is intellectual contraception. To think
and not nurture the idea is intellectual abortion.

Men, when they think and teach, are reproducing spiritual life. This is the normal thing to do whether you have
attended Normal School or not. Mankind needs ideas more
than it needs bread. The man, then, who thinks and gives to
others the fruits of his thinking is repaying his indebtedness
to mankind in a mature way.

To paraphrase [Eric] Gill's famous remark, the thinker is
not a special kind of man, but every man is a special kind of
thinker.

We do have, however, along with the common garden
variety of thinker, the man who devotes his life to tending
ideas much as other men might devote their time to tending
sheep. These intellectuals and scholars provide a tremendously
valuable function in society. This job is not, as is sometimes
supposed, to do the thinking for the rest of us, but rather to
make sure that the treasury of human wisdom be sustained
and nurtured to greater growth. Where the average man's
thought are about local and specific matters, these men deal
with the essence of things and universals. Thus they maintain intact a kind of convoy that accompanies man in his
voyage through time, carrying spiritual food, protecting him
from ignorance, providing man with a lifeline from where
he is to where he is going.

The third form of human reproduction is art. Few words have suffered more the ravages of sloppy thinking. Art is best defined as human skill in making, whether it be bridges or phrases, false teeth or tables, solariums or sonnets. The act of production through human skill can only be analogously termed a reproduction of life. There is, we must admit, an invaluable something in everything made by the craftsman which is a part of himself. When a man makes something, he expresses a certain life that is within him, and the thing made is used to facilitate the life of others. When an artist takes his raw materials (a baker may take wheat, yeast, water and salt; a poet may take nouns, pronouns and verbs) the order that he gives to these materials comes from him. The order of bread or a sonnet is not in the parts. The order is in the maker. He puts this order in his work, and it is this order that the user abstracts from the thing made. The man who by his effort makes the things that sustain the life of the body and the life of the spirit is a mature man. He is discharging in an honorable way his indebtedness to mankind.

The fourth form of reproductivity, apostolicity, will be considered a bit later.

The Current Sterility

These three categories of human reproductivity supply us with an excellent criterion by which to measure modern society. Merely to describe them as I have done here is practically a condemnation of the current scene, for is it not, in fact, these very categories of activity that are the most sadly neglected in our time?

Give a Look

The idea of marrying and the idea of having children no

longer necessarily presuppose each other. You are indeed presumptuous if you presume that married people are going to have children. Nor is it considered polite to ask. The most sought-after bit of information by engaged couples is how to avoid having children. Let's not labor that point. It is, however, the focal point, the consequence and the cause of widespread immaturity. That the modern rejects the minimum biological responsibility of propagating the race, is certainly a measure of our degradation.

It is not so easy to prove that there is a conspiracy against the intellectual life, but no proof is necessary if you by any chance have been attempting to encourage thinking among your neighbors. Whether you are a parish priest, a school teacher, a unionist, a soapbox orator, a member of a family group, a student, or just an ordinary Joe, if you have tried lately to get a group of people together to think a problem through, then I don't need to tell you that it's a lost art. Circumstantial evidence can be submitted in the way of adult comic books, photographic magazines, the half-thought-out glibness of popular commentators, the scarcity of intelligent opinion, the ubiquity of the greeting card, the toleration of moronic politicians and beyond this, the rabid anti-intellectualism found in many quarters of society where a thinker is regarded with malignant distrust.

Every conversation in the observation car or in the factory lunchroom is a warmed-over collection of mass-produced opinions. How few people there are who feel an urgency to stop and think, and how great the legions who flee the prospect! It is seldom that a moralist will raise the question of sloth in the midst of flagrant intellectual laziness, yet to let our minds grow flabby is much more reprehensible than physical sloth, and it is certainly a greater obstacle to virtue.

Sterile Activity

To say that we do not want babies does not imply that we are continent people. Quite the contrary! To say that we do not want ideas, does not mean that we are an uninquisitive people. Equally to the contrary! We are prone to abortive copulation, and for the same reason we are prone to a sterile inquisitiveness. Sex indulgence is the great pleasure of the body. Intellectual curiosity is the great pleasure of the mind. The latter no more implies ideas than the former implies babies.

Collecting facts is a fetish which has a superficial resemblance to scholarship. There is no more reason for thinking a fact-collector is a thinker than to conclude that a rag collector is a tailor. Facts are the raw material for ideas, but they have an enchantment all their own and once we become enamored, the likelihood that an idea will emerge becomes very slight. The research man, the factologist, is according to our definition, intellectually immature. Much like a child, his concern for things distracts from the possibility of his making anything. His interest is not in living reality and dynamic creativity. His concern is for carefully embalmed corpses, each placed on its little slab and filed away in a well-indexed morgue. The fraud that is being perpetrated here cannot be condemned too strongly. The common man has come to put his trust in science, looking to the laboratory for leadership. He takes for granted that these men are safeguarding society from ignorance, and are guiding our national and cosmic affairs in a discreet and reasonable fashion. He placed his hopes for the future in these serious young men who move about inscrutably with their briefcases or mumble quietly over their slide-rules. It would appear that all of these very clever people had the situation well in hand. The contrary is true.

The inquiry into all the various blind forces of nature, whether the object of inquiry be atomic power, sex or the law of supply and demand, up to now has been done at the price of life, whether it be the life of the body, of the mind of the soul, or of society. Subsequent to their various triumphs the scientists announce some particular benefit to life that may come as a consequence of their research. This is just grandstanding. It has nothing to do with the game. The search is for verification, not truth. The concern is for power, not life.

The average man remains intellectually immature because he has been persuaded by the experts, with their mumbo-jumbo and bags full of facts, that he hasn't the intelligence to think for himself. The experts, in turn, betray a constant immaturity by persevering in research, invention and therapy, unconcerned for the whole truth, the life. The unleashing of the atomic bomb, for example, was not the act of criminals, but of children. They were not intellectually or responsibly "old enough to know better."

The Machine Tender

The average modern worker is not an artist but a machine tender, and in this fact lies the difference between maturity and immaturity. If, as Christians, we are concerned about the condition of the working classes, it is not only in respect to their material welfare, but even more in solicitude that their work be an instrument for developing virtue. Industrialism is not concerned with the welfare of the worker at all. This lack of consideration is exhibited in the worker's having been stripped of property, forced to live in sub-human quarters, but most of all by eliminating in him the need for skill or the development of human virtues.

The average worker, male or female, is required to do

work for eight hours each day which, by no stretch of the imagination would he choose to do had he a choice in the matter. No child in dreaming of his future has ever longed for the day when he might type from dawn to dusk, make the same limited repetitious gesture forty hours a week, drive an elevator up and down continuously, or file cards in pigeon holes *ad infinitum.* He has dreamed of being some kind of planner and maker, and perfecter of things. This latter dream has been denied except to a fortunate few. Thus work has come to be looked upon as a slavery, and the object of all effort is the pursuit of leisure.

Such a condition is a guarantee of immaturity. Why? Because the prerequisite to maturity is a sense of responsibility. The precise opposite to an artist (a responsible worker) is an automaton (a machine). The most essential industrial worker (except those few who are in the planning and designing departments) is the irresponsible man, the automaton. This irresponsibility must be cultivated in the worker because the asymmetrical rhythm of human virtue is antagonistic to the symmetrical rhythm of the machine. If this statement is too abstract, let me make it clearer by saying that courtesy, charity, ingenuity, spontaneity, recollection, tact and any other human virtue you may name, are all monkey wrenches in the wheel of technological progress. The courteous bus driver will miss his schedule and fumble his change. The ingenious screw-machine operator will slow down his production time ("We have a man who is paid to be ingenious"). The charitable commuter will be late for work. The just truck driver will betray his company by giving place to weaker fellow workers. The tactful file clerk (tact is the virtue by which you give everything its just due) will be slowed down by his disdain for trivia (trivia is the largest category in most filing departments).

To fit into the process the worker gradually develops a deafness to the inner voice. Every time he responded in the past to his conception of right and wrong, truth and error, proportion and disproportion, he upset the boss, lost a sale, missed a train, insulted a co-worker, broke the machine, or typed the wrong address. So he became adapted, he learned to like his work. The price he paid was his sense of responsibility.

Unfortunately (for, were it otherwise, the solution would be easy), a man cannot be both a responsible man and an irresponsible man at one and the same time, so his after-hour activities and his off-the-job obligations reflect the irresponsibility so assiduously cultivated. He does not want to work, he does not want children, he does not want to think, because were he to do any of these he would embark upon a voyage of responsible maturity, filled with all of those unknown terrors from which the machine, the boss, the state and the buck have protected him.

The Emerging Pattern

Out of this study a certain pattern becomes apparent. It would seem that men have become preoccupied with the processes of living at the expense of life itself. This would be a contradiction if it were not a paradox. It is a paradox with which any Christian should be familiar. We have heard the words, "He who would gain his life must lose it." If we cling tenaciously to the life processes, what we wear, what we put on, what we can prove, what we desire, what we can produce, we do not gain life but become sterile. Preoccupation with sex is making the family barren. Preoccupation with facts is atrophying the intellect. Preoccupation with production is making us unskilled automatons, and depleting our natural resources. We love our lives so much we lack the capacity for sacrifice, and thus remain children.

Self-sacrifice and the mortification of desire are the prerequisites if one is to be a mature custodian over life. The parent dies daily that the child may live. The idealist becomes a martyr so that his idea will become fertilized with his blood. The craftsman grows bent and calloused in service. They die and yet they live in the fruits of their giving.

The life of the race, of the intellect and of the culture cannot survive unless it is incorporated into a divine Life. There must be some higher life, some greater happiness that makes the sacrifice of this human life worthwhile. A man will only be generous with his life, if in losing it, he gains a higher life. No branch will bear fruit if it is separated from the vine. Men will be immature and barren until they are engrafted on Christ.

This is a Caricature

I was once accused by a very courteous questioner in Chicago of resorting to the same kind of caricature in my articles as I do in my cartoons. I admit to this fact. A caricature is the delineation of a pattern in which significant facts are exaggerated, and from which insignificant facts are excluded. That would be an apt description of this article. The cartoonist provides his audience with merely a frame upon which each can build his own structure. This, I think, is more complimentary to the reader than the work of a scholar who not only builds your entire edifice for you, but also sends you the hinges, door knobs and over-drape hooks wrapped up in his footnotes.

Now when a cartoonist makes a drawing of a saint, the last thing he does is to draw in the halo. This is not something merely added to the figure, as one might add a hat, but it is a sign that symbolizes a new quality that transfigures the entire portrait. The halo signifies a qualitative change in the subject of the cartoon. What was at first the drawing of a natural man is now a picture of a man infused with divine grace.

The prose-picture drawn cartoon fashion in this article has been that of human maturity, its definition and an analysis of the social evils that stand as obstacles in its way. If I now add to this a fourth kind of productivity, aspostolicity, I am not merely adding a hat but a halo. The entire quality of my subject will be transfigured. The facts which might have provoked despair become infused with hope. What might appear to have been a stalemate now becomes a challenge. No longer is it merely a question of man repaying his debt to the species through parenthood, thought and art, but man doing precisely the same things but now as part of a divine mission, infused with Christ-life, tasting of inevitable triumph.

Apostolicity

Because Christ has redeemed us and given us a share in His life and mission through the Sacraments, we now assume a new responsibility when we speak of maturity. We have the privilege of propagating the Christ-life. This does not exclude the other forms of reproductivity but assumes them into a higher end and more glorious purpose. Rather than lessening the importance of parenthood, thought, and responsible work, these now become sacredly significant.

That is why the current lack of Christian apostolicity overshadows all other social problems. Since it has been designed by God as the end to which all the powers of man should be turned, and since within its scope all forms of reproductivity become more bountiful, and since it is the current which leads all mankind to God and eternal happiness, in embracing apostolicity we are indeed restoring all life to Christ.

Apostolic reproductivity is not by our powers, but by the power of God. Consequently those adverse social circumstances I outlined before which are obstacles to human maturity, become for the apostle not obstacles but occasions for maturation. If parenthood has become more and more difficult, due to economic pressure and social stigma, we can embrace it to bring more souls to Christ and this thing we accept as a cross becomes a lever by which we can pry other couples free. Once freed of their fears and trusting in God they can go on to change the economic order, making it comply with the needs of the family. If thinking has become obsolete, we can embrace it, learning the mind of the Church, gaining self-knowledge and the knowledge of man. Then, with this weapon forged in fire we can set others free to find Truth, Who is Christ. If responsible workmanship has become extinct, we can bear the cross of slavery throughout the day, and seek in our leisure to gain mastery of tools. These skills are needed to implement the work of decentralization, restoring property, providing homes, publishing pamphlets, enhancing the liturgy, restoring the ill and the insane. From such skill applied in an organized fashion, new social institutions will emerge to displace the over-crowded city, the proletarian apartments, the pornographic pulps, the mass-production factories, the passive congregations and the medical abattoirs. Thus we are faced with a privilege we dare not refuse: to be grown-ups in Christ.

MEN, MARY, AND MANLINESS

Ed Willock

Manliness is the masculine virtue that makes the man best adapted to achieving a common goal with the partnership of woman, ultimately to save souls. When a man permits other interests to make him ignore his responsibilities to others, he is unmanly. Husband and wife must work more closely together than ever before.

Not so long ago, it was customary among the unpretentious to refer to a strange or perverse view of things as being "cockeyed." As many other popular expression, this had a certain magical profundity and aptness. No doubt it was coined by some unremembered Shakespeare. We do see so many views today that are undoubtedly "cockeyed," if by cockeyed we mean that one eye has capitulated or gone over to the other. In the mad scheme of things that philosophers recognize as normal, each human eye has a certain autonomy of its own. Even though they are side by side in the same head, nature has given to either eye a right to its own opinion. The mind, of course, being in a position of command accepts the two opinions submitted, grateful for the fact that there is a somewhat different view from either side of the nose, and from the composite picture draws its own conclusions. When the eyes are cocked, each is jealous and inquisitively invading the domain of the other. Each eye is acting as though the other had no right to exist. As though, like the ancient Cyclops, nature might have done better by placing one eye, autocratically enthroned, in the middle of the forehead.

I think that there were reasons other than whimsy in God's decision to give us two eyes rather than one. After much thought I have concluded that in the omnipotent opinion of the Creator, we could see better that way. Whatever it is that eyes are meant to do, they can do it best as mates, each with a certain autonomy, each with its own way of looking at things, and each careful that its eager inquisitiveness does not invade the domain of the other. The same divine judiciousness was exercised at the time when Adam was relieved of a superfluous rib and the race of mankind suddenly became bi-partisan. I think we can draw with a certain resignation, if not with enthusiasm, the conclusion that whatever it is that God wishes the human race to accomplish, He wants it to be the mutual collaboration of two parties. Each party must make its own peculiar contribution. Each must respect the domain of the other. Both must cooperate. Mankind cannot accomplish its mission in a merely masculine way, nor can it accomplish it in a merely feminine way. The mission will be a common striving for a common goal. Men and women need each other in order to be man.

My left eye and my right eye do different jobs, but the jobs are to the same end, and they work together. If my eyes refuse to work together, a state of ocular anarchy ensues and I become "walleyed." If one insists upon usurping the perogatives of the other, I become "cockeyed." The normal state of ocular health then can be described as a mutual tension which sets them apart, and an opposing tension that draws them together. These tensions of attraction and repulsion produce a certain equilibrium, a certain appropriate harmony of operation. A comparable condition of attraction and repulsion exists between the human sexes. It is normal for a man to love a woman: this is the attraction. A man does not want to become a woman; this is the repulsion. It is the same with the woman. The condition that is to be desired is an equilibrium of opposing forces. When we find this satisfactory and happy condition in a woman, we say she is womanly. When we find it in a man, we say he is manly. Manliness, then, is the masculine virtue that makes the man best adapted to achieving a common goal with the collaboration of women. As Christians we recognize that goal as the saving of our several souls, and the making of temporal institutions which will further that end.

We Need an Ideal Woman

It is impossible to measure a straight line with a crooked yardstick. Ever since Eve went shopping through Eden in search of a new delicacy and accepted the tasty morsel proffered by Satan, she, Adam, and their innumerable children have been prone to invent their own standards of conduct. The closets of history are packed with crooked yardsticks, abandoned by the generation which followed after those who said the crooked could measure the straight. Each generation has its own fanciful measure of manliness and womanliness. Both Caesar's wife and Napoleon's mistress have enjoyed short reigns as symbols of womanliness. In America we can see subtle contrasts between such ideals as the pioneer mother and Miss America. Trekking across the prairies of the West seemed to demand different virtues from those required to tread the boardwalk at Atlantic City. The costumes as well as the customs of the two periods have few points in common.

If, then, Caesar, Napoleon, the pioneer husband, and Mr. America achieved a fairly workable relationship with their various mates, it would seem that we are provided with diverse and contradictory examples of manliness. If manliness is to be measured in reference to women, we must have some symbol of womanliness that is both imminent in the affairs of history and yet transcends the changing pattern of human perversity. Such a woman must be a living human being adapting herself to the good that lives in every page of history. She must at the same time reign transcendent, immutable in her radiant perfection. We have such a woman, and her name is Mary. She is a virgin, and yet a mother. She is an active housewife, and yet a contemplative, a mystic. She walks upon the stars, and yet it is her delight to be with the children of men. She was seen in the dusk of the setting Testament by Simeon the prophet. She was seen yesterday at high noon by three children of Portugal. With a certainty for which most men will die and after which few reporters will seek, we know that she is with us, in all our affairs, Mary, the mother of Christ and our mother.

We Must Know Mary

It is a healthy sign for the increase of manliness that a true devotion to Mary is being so widely propagated today. The Mary to whom I was introduced in parochial school and to whom I prayed in childhood and who, I am sure, is the concept held by most Catholics today, though an admirable Mary, is a person somewhat less grand, and somewhat more fuzzy than the Mary of the Gospels.

As I conceived of her then, she was a sort of mid-Victorian maiden-lady of means. It would have been difficult to see her in the role of a busy, work-strained mother of the kitchen. The role best suited to her would have been that of an angelically benevolent social worker, who would sit serenely in the parlor, sympathetic, compassionate, but never quite immersed in our mundane problems.

That, at least, was the idea I got. I had the impression that she disliked most of the dirty sins, which I later came to realize were the Protestant sins: drinking, smoking, uncleanliness, profanity and impurity. Of course as time went on, I found out that the Church had a somewhat different hierarchy of vices and virtues from these. The Mary whom I had been led to revere suffered in the interpretation. Teachers and parents to whom I am undyingly grateful for their exemplary virtue, boloxed up the doctrine quite a bit trying to get it into our stupid little heads, and added to it liberal spoonfuls of their own Irish puritanism. Unfortunately for many Catholics, this is the only idea of Mary that they have. It is difficult for men with such a view of Mary to see the relevance of her life to mature manliness. "Little men," they recall, "always sit up straight, keep their hands folded, never curse or swear, and especially never think, talk, or act as though there were any such thing as (blush) girls." I realize, of course, that from sheer necessity Catholic men have had to revise this concept of Mary to meet the changing circumstances of their relations with women, but the revision has been a patch-up job unaided by theological accuracy.

Today, there is ample literature inspired on the most part by the fruitful apostolate of St. Louis de Montfort, to provide any man who desires it, with a mature understanding of the doctrine of Mary, as well as the occasion for becoming, in truth, her son in Christ. Manliness, then, can best be determined in reference to a true understanding and a true devotion to Mary.

A Lesson from Cana

For the purposes of this brief essay I have chosen to write about the relations between the sexes other than the marital act. Manliness in regards to this act is, of course, of utmost importance and is most certainly related to Mary. Manliness in husbands can never be measured apart from their conduct as lovers, and a failure to see the relevance of Mary to this act lies at the root of current marital unhappiness. I do not pass over this briefly because it is unimportant, but rather because it is too important and too misunderstood to be dealt with other than intimately and cautiously. Prudence and prudery should never be confused even though they may sound alike. There are other numerous relationships between men and women, both married and single, to which an understanding of manliness and Mary can well apply. More and more, women today are taking equal part in common enterprises with men. It is obvious that a greater collaboration between wives and husbands is needed today than was customary in the past. Manliness must be understood in all of these relations if they are to meet with harmony and success.

The story of the marriage feast at Cana is providing a good deal of inspiration to apostolic marriage groups today. Many are the lessons to be drawn from it. There is one lesson, however, that is especially relevant to my article. Cana stands at mid-noon between the dawn at Bethlehem and the dusk of Calvary. It is a turning point in the epic of the Incarnation. At a time when Christ is shown to us in His most human aspect, as a guest at a marriage feast, He gives a breathtaking evidence of His divinity. Much as a kindly neighbor might help out a distracted host by repairing a bothersome electric toaster, Christ helped the party to come off, and at the same time proved His divinity to His followers, by changing water into wine. The magnificent gesture suffered not at all, but was rather enhanced, by the circumstances under which it was performed. It was the act of a God Who was, at the same time, a friendly neighbor.

The conversation that went on between Jesus and Mary at that time is most revealing. Mary noticed the embarrassment of the host and said simply, "They have no wine." Christ answered just as simply, "Woman, what is that to thee and to Me? My hour is not yet come." Our Lord's words, we are advised, suffer in translation. "Woman," as a title in those days, was both courteous and proper. The rest of His statement could be translated as "Never mind," or, "Don't bother about it." The time was not yet ripe for Him to demonstrate His divine powers. Apparently Mary read more in His looks that we can determine from the words. She undoubtedly expected Him to comply when she said to the waiters, "Whatsoever He shall say to you, do ye." We are all familiar with the consequent miracle.

The rather nice thing about this episode is the demonstration of the complementary nature of manliness and womanliness. As a lesson for us it casts Christ and Mary in the role of man and woman, seemingly endowing each with peculiar weaknesses which we know in reality they do not possess. In this little drama, Christ appears to have that social obtuseness common to the male. It tickles a man to think that Christ might not have noticed the discomfort of the host. How like a man! Husbands can recall so frequently a wifely kick in the shins to remind them that an air of gloom has descended on the gathering. Mrs. Brophy, who dislikes cigars, is sitting next to Uncle Al and his inevitable stogie. Mrs. Bagby, who lives at the other side of town, is trying to catch her husband's eye to remind him that the last bus leaves in ten minutes.

On the other hand, Mary, in the story of Cana, seems to have forgotten the cosmic significance of her Son's mission. Should He, Who is about to embark upon the salvation of mankind, be bothered by the trifling matter of a *faux pas?* How like a woman! Mr. Jones is in the midst of setting the center span of the George Washington Bridge in place and he gets a phone call from his wife reminding him not to forget to bring home some paper napkins for little Marjorie's birthday party. Mr. Pazinski is working on the last movement of his first symphony, and his wife comes in and asks him to remind the milkman not to leave three quarts of milk today because Wilfred is going to stay overnight at Aunt Agatha's.

At this point in the story we see a complication, which daily has plagued the affairs of mankind since the dawn of time. We see a certain tension existing between the man's concern about missions and the woman's concern about persons. Let us see how Mary and Jesus resolved this complication before we go into its significance for us.

It would seem that Christ reversed His decision from one of refusal to one of compliance. This, I believe, was done for our benefit. First it gave us striking evidence of the intercessional powers of Mary, Mediatrix. Christ, the Omnipotent and the Omniscient, is moved by a word from Mary. The second lesson is one that is related to my thesis here. Christ must have seen a relevance between this minor catastrophe of failing wine and His major epic of Salvation, or else He would not have performed the miracle, nor would Mary have asked Him to do so. For our edification He countered His question, "What does it matter?" with the answer, "It does matter!" The simple trifles of daily life, kindly concerns, the niceties of neighborliness, in other words, the flesh of life, are part and parcel with the epic of the Cross and the

Sword. The mission of Christ, the mission within which all our missions find their validity, embraces all things fondly; as Chesterton expresses it: "But one thing is necessary—everything!"

It is a matter of universal observation, as well as a lesson from Cana, that men are by the nature of masculinity, fondly concerned with things. Not only are they concerned as craftsmen with steel and wood and cement and pipes, but as philosophers and organizers with the less tangible things of causes, techniques, and theories. Women, on the other hand, are most fondly concerned with persons, and when they are concerned with things, it is only as they are relevant to persons. The fact that these interests overlap does not take away from the fact that the male and female perspectives are different, but only proves that the differences are meant to be complementary. Just as the two views of an object seen by either eye unite in the mind to provide a full-rounded, three-dimensional figure, so also do the male and female perspectives combine to supply mankind with a full-rounded view of reality from which to make his judgements. Just as the left eye may perceive from its corner a danger the right eye might overlook, so, too, does the female soul respond to a portent that the male may fail to see. Man's is the perspective of things. Woman's is the perspective of persons. The composite of these two views is as close to a full perception of reality as man can achieve.

Unmanliness

When a man permits his interest in things to make him ignore his responsibilities to persons, he is unmanly. Whenever this is the case it is the woman who suffers, because he is, in fact, violating the things which she holds sacred, or else interfering with her operation within that area. If, for example, the Don Juan were to consider for a time that the women he uses as playthings are indeed persons, and if he were aware of how personally the ladies, no matter how loose, were wounded by his momentary passion, the obligation of male celibacy and marital fidelity would seem to him much more incumbent upon human nature. God has endowed the man with a certain objectivity so that he can reason without passion and thus move swiftly and surely to truth and justice. It is this same objectivity that can turn to abuse when the man insists upon eliminating the personal factor, treating everything personal as an intrusion upon his work, or reducing persons to integers in his own pet equation.

Some Catholic historians have conceded to the adverse critics of the Middle Ages that the people of those times were more brutal than the modern man. I think that is conceding too much. I think it is less brutal to sever the head of an enemy with a cross-sword, than to fire an innocent employee by means of an interoffice memo. At least in the Middle Ages great caution was taken to safeguard the noncombatant women and children. Ours is the brutality of Hiroshima, where a comparatively well-dressed man, deliberately, and with little need for courage, pressed a button which brought screaming death about the ears of grandmothers and babes in arms. Manliness is not in the stomach, but in the mind. The modern stomach may revolt against the stake and sword of the Middle Ages, but our minds can adapt themselves quite nicely to remote injustices for which we are responsible. Yes, perhaps our stomachs are more delicate. That is why we must drive our cars quickly through the areas of the city that bear the marks of our commercial brutality so that we may pacify our stomachs with the civilized gentility of the suburbs.

The brutality by remote control that characterizes the

present generation is the fruit of a tradition which was masculinely dominated. Women have always been the trustees of human life and the stewards of human dignity. When Mary was revered by men in their works and politics, they conducted their affairs with due respect for the woman, the family and for human life. If in the days of Mary women were confined to the home, they were confined not as prisoners, but as queens. Yesterday's theory has been supported by today's fact, that a woman stands beside a man more proudly as a wife than as a secretary. History testifies to the fact that homes were sacred when the leaders of nations stood in cruel armor beneath the banners of the Virgin, and now, when the leaders stand neatly in business suits beneath emblems of their own devising, the cities of the world, whether bombed or bomb-free, have heaped their families in sorry piles. Only yesterday I saw the forlorn sight of a mother and child, huddled in an airless and sunless New York room, watching across the street a long stretch of river bank being cleared so that the men in business suits in the U.N. could comfortably discuss the lack of housing in the world.

In the areas where ideas are manufactured, we see the same perverse masculinity and unmanliness. The saints and scholars to whom we are indebted for our traditional Catholic thought, always did their work in the company of Mary. Neither God nor man ever became for them a mere theory or fact. God was always a Person, and man was a person unto His Image. The entire universe was a personal message from God to man. Thus their logic and objectivity, though pure and dispassionate, were always related to their love of the divine Persons. When Mary, the Seat of Wisdom, was expelled from the schools and in her place they erected the idol of Pure Reason, the much-boasted rationality of the thinkers soon became irrationality. They might have been saved from this madness if they had not divorced their academics from the realm of personal life. Had they only regarded persons instead of theories for a while, they would have seen the suicides, neuroses, irresponsibilities, infidelities, and homosexualities of the poor souls who applied their warped ideas to human behavior. Had they interspersed their ratiocinations with the quiet contemplation of a Marian Magnificat, the Holy Ghost would have readjusted the focus of their inquiry. They would have learned from Mary that Truth and Love are One, and He is Christ. Where there is not charity there cannot be truth.

Mary does not accompany the modern man in his studies nor in his work. In the realm of ideas, he scorns her passive humility, her contemplative wisdom. In business he rejects as sentimentalism her tears for the weak and the oppressed. In politics he does not live with justice as she did, nor does he clothe the common good as she did. That is why homes and babies, and all the other delicate matters of human dignity which are dear to the hearts of women, are looked upon as bothersome intrusions in the machinery of progress. So obtuse is the modern male in his unmanliness, that he honestly believes that this technical heaven he has built is a blessing to womankind. He cannot see that the glamour and gadgets are second-rate substitutes for dignified womanhood and babies.

While at Home

At home the process is reversed. Without Mary, the natural hierarchy of Nazareth has toppled. Mama and Junior battle it out to see which is going to run Daddy. It is not uncommon to hear of a shrewd enterpriser who scorns the supine whimpers of his employees begging for more wages, lavishing his wealth upon an indolent son and a demanding wife, slave to their every whim and fancy. He is a ruthless tyrant at his desk and a maudlin old lady in his home. This pattern of dual control is repeated all the way down through the income layers of the social cake. The taxi driver that rides the road like Attila the Hun, washes the dishes at home so that his teenage daughters won't mar their paint job. Men who cannot tolerate weakness in their co-workers are quite satisfied to leave it up to mama to raise a race of juvenile softies.

The unmanliness of economic, philosophic and political brutality has its counterpart in the home where manliness abdicates so that feminine sentimentality and neurosis can rule the roost. Because she is without a head, the little woman is turning to fashions and bridge, coffee and cigarettes, trying to find the solace and dignity that can only be hers as mate to a man who has a dignified mission, which he hopes to impart to her children. Instead of providing her with an ideal and with children, he feeds her hunger with orchids and furs. He could never be so cruel as to burden her with the cross of salvation.

From Mary these men could learn that charity is austere. Although she suffered in every fiber the indignities and brutality directed against her Son, Mary never for a moment discouraged Him in His awful mission, but rather reared Him in austere preparation for it.

From men is expected the directives of justice and austerity and though they must be careful not to ride roughshod over the sensibilities of womankind, they cannot capitulate to women without losing their manliness.

Working Together

Manliness is important in the lay apostolate. Our mission as men will be worked out in close collaboration with

the women. The family apostolate has learned from experience that the husband and wife must work more closely together than has been the traditional custom. At first the men
may feel that having the women around is a handicap. I used
to think so myself, but I have learned that whether it be a
family movement or a project consisting of single people,
the contribution of the ladies is exactly what is needed to
complement the efforts of the men. The women are bringing into public life and private discussion the qualities of
Mary, and it is these qualities that are most needed, and beside which a new manliness can grow.

To cite a few examples: The idea of personal sanctification cannot be divorced from any apostolate. We cannot give
what we haven't got. Men may be firmly convinced of the
need for sanctity, but it is the women who will add to this
conviction a devout conversion of the will. Men are attracted
by the idea of sanctity, but the women, practical creatures
that they are, transmit the ideas from the head to the knees.
Sanctity, while there are women around, means prayers, fasts
and good works.

When women are present, men are less liable to indulge
in endless debate. Women introduce that little bit of whim-
sical anarchy which is an antidote for pompous logic. The
concern of the ladies is for persons, not syllogisms.

Women will temper the self-sufficiency of the men with
their innate and constant dependence upon God. Sure, men
want God as a partner but they tend to reduce Him to the
level of a co-partner or a junior partner. Because the women
have learned gracefully to take a back seat all through the
ages, they are less liable to forget Who is driving the universe. When the women take part, God's primacy and His
Providence will be a prominent consideration in every judgment.

Finally, when it comes to action, the ladies will see to the welfare of the innocent. They will be concerned for the toes that might be stepped on. Because they are more sensitive to the feelings of persons, they can teach men many lessons in human kindness and the power of persuasion.

Manliness, then, will grow in reference to Mary. Devotion to her will make for an effective collaboration with women. It will save us from the two extremes of brutality and effeminacy. And don't think for a moment that I think the problem is resolved because it is down on paper. The equilibrium between the sexes is a much more difficult one to achieve or to maintain than the equilibrium between the eyes. The thing involved here is the most ornery of God's creatures, the human will. I am tempted to add a line to the famous quotation of Pope Pius XI: "All men have the imperative duty to remember that they have a mission to fulfill, that of doing the impossible—collaborating with women." With Christ and Mary, however, "all things are possible."

THE FAMILY HAS LOST ITS HEAD

Ed Willock

Marriage is a happy relationship because of the difference between the sexes, not because they are similar. Differences in being mean difference of status. Men and women are clearly different physically and psychologically. These differences combine to make the man the leader in any household. The two causes for the failure of men to lead their family are 1)female immodesty and male incontinence, and 2)the man's intellectual irresponsibility.

The rhyme about Mr. and Mrs. Jack Sprat and their divergent tastes in meat is a refreshing relic from some earlier day when it was considered more important that mates should be complementary than that they should be similar. The fact that Jack could eat no fat and the Mrs. eat no lean, is as apt and typical a condition of marital dissimilarity as one could find. My wife abhors sugar in her tea, whereas I dislike cream. My friend's wife loves brilliantly colored furnishings, while he prefers neutral shades. This divergence in tastes, rather than making married life difficult, is the factor most contributive to its preservation as an institution. Diversity makes for beauty.

In this factor we see but one in a legion of reasons why the idea of the family and the true relation of its parts is almost incomprehensible to the modern mind. In the modern scheme of things the concept of unity is not that which one finds in an organism such as a flower or a vine, but rather that kind of unity found in a heap of ashes. Instead of dissimilar things brought to a common fruition by a sharing of functions, the modern unity is achieved by the reduction of all things to their elemental form. The relations of persons is no longer a meeting of minds, but a wedding of valences, or, in marriage, the reconciliation of metabolisms. Consequently the solution to divorce is not the marriage of likes, but marriage based upon a concept of life that finds order and beauty in diversity. The sole requirement for pairing off under such a concept would be that the man be manly, the woman, womanly, and both more or less willing to accept the fact that the children would be childish. All that needs to be common to a man and wife is a common Faith, common sense, a common bed and board, and common children. Beyond this, all other common interests can only cement the marital bond, if they are interests normally common to either sex.

To the peril of the institution of the family, men are seeking to build the common bond upon those habits of the man and woman, which by their nature should remain autonomous. Rarely sharing a common Faith, the marital expert insists that the mates read the same books or smoke the same brand of cigarettes. Commonly lacking common sense, the man and wife are counseled to share the same intellectual prejudices. Frequently lacking a normal quota of common children, the couples are advised to baby each other, and play the same games. Now if the basis of marriage harmony is playing the same games, you may be sure that it will be a losing game, and one in which it will be more and more the custom for one child to pick up the marbles and look for another playmate. To say that marriage is companionship is the same kind of lie as saying that Christ was a good man. If that is all that He is, or all that it is, then the human race has been victim of a malicious fraud. If marriage is a question of a man leaving a number of male companions to cling to one female companion, then marriage is a mad institution indeed. It is just a mad kind of card game in which the dummy has the children; it is a kind of tennis match in which the children are the balls and love is a way of keeping score. It is a race in which the human race is bound to lose.

Marriage is a wonderful thing that only God could have invented. The Church compares it with the union between Christ and His Church, for there is no other comparison on earth to do it justice. This should serve as warning to us that we should approach a study of marriage with great humility, realizing at the outset that this institution has only the faintest resemblance to the modern substitute falsely classified under the same title, and listed in the same book at City Hall.

Saint Paul has something to say about marriage which is of more than passing interest. The Church, in her wisdom, has incorporated it into the nuptial Mass. The good saint says, "Let women be subject to their husbands as to the Lord: for the husband is the head of the wife, as Christ is the Head of the Church. He is the Savior of His body; therefore, as the Church is subject to Christ, so let the wives be to their husbands in all things." On the basis of this testimony, with that nasty dogmatism so characteristic of Catholics, I present the statement without debate that "the man is head of the family." This is a conclusion hardly substantiated by statistics. Generally speaking, the American male is not the head of the family. This difference between the counsel of St. Paul and the evidences of our senses in the matter of masculine headship is of prime importance, if we are intent upon reforming the family. The restoration of all things in Christ must include, well up on the agenda, the restoring of the man to his proper position within the family economy.

The Differences Between the Sexes

The most obvious fact and consequently the one most overlooked except by simpleminded Christians, is that marriage is a happy relationship because of the difference between the sexes, and not because they are similar. The proper end of marriage is the propagation of children and depends, it has been whispered, on functions peculiar to each sex. This evokes a problem very upsetting to the equalitarian. Difference of function implies difference of status. You cannot say that a woman is the equal of a man, any more than you can say that an apple is the equal of a peach, unless you have a different definition of equality from the rest of mankind. This difference between the sexes is not only physical, but also psychological, and it is because of these natural differences, and not because of any ecclesiastical decree that man is the normal head of the family.

Man's physical qualifications for the job of headship are seldom questioned. His superior physical strength makes him the logical breadwinner, and for obvious reasons the breadwinner should be the head of the family. Women, during long periods of pregnancy and while nursing, are dependent. This dependency indicates the function of the man. The head of the family must be independent. Adequate as these reasons may be for the establishment of headship, it is more the psychological peculiarities of the man which indicate his proper function as husband and father.

The outstanding male tendency is to be objective. The man can more readily stand off and consider a thing apart from its relation to himself. In a woman this quality, though possible, is rarely developed. She, on the contrary, is personal and tends to measure all things with her heart. For that reason she is more readily sympathetic and willing to serve. It is this tendency, when brought to virtue, which makes a woman the warm, pulsating heart of the family. When she is free to do so, a woman gravitates to certain interests and occupations different from those which capture the fancy of man. Seldom is she interested in those sciences which demand the utmost in objectivity. The fields of theology, philosophy, mathematics and academic law have been, and always will be, the fields of the man. Anything which requires human sympathy and selfless friendship will be most attractive to women. Women succeed as novelists, on the whole, because of their easily stimulated sympathies, and wherever the male novelist is superior, it is usually because of philosophic content. Since man's objectivity makes him more interested in universals than particulars, the composition of music and the making of art objects in their purest form, will always be predominantly male occupations. It is neither by accident nor conspiracy that women have always been homemakers, nor is it male arrogance to say that that is their proper place. The female temperament is most happy surrounded by particular and familiar creatures on which she may be free to exercise her tremendous capacity for loving devotion.

To tell a man that he is illogical is as much an insult as to deny a woman's intuitive abilities. Wives will always say, "John Jones, you make me mad. You're always so coldly analytical!" The husband will eternally retort, "But you are always jumping to conclusions!" This is the method proper to each for attaining a deeper understanding of truth. The combination of the logical genius of man and the intuitive genius of woman is one of God's most beautiful syntheses, and it is the natural gift upon which the parents' authority to teach the children is based.

Man's other tendencies are a consequence of his objectivity, and his physical prowess. He is by nature aggressive and direct. It is his to initiate and to envision. The woman is by nature more retiring, satisfied to find strength in her husband's protection. She is circumspect, using devious methods to gain her ends, resorting to tact or diplomacy as expedient instruments. All of these innate characteristics help us to determine man's proper place in society and in the home.

Difficult to Prove

What I have said here is not all that can be said about the relation of the man and wife in marriage, and you can't prove any of it by the isolated case of John Dee or Mary Daa. It would be even difficult to prove the aptness of categorizing male and female temperaments in this way, by taking a poll among your friends. That is the sad part of it! There is a condition in modern times which, for lack of a better word, I will call feminization. It is a condition both in the family and in the community which is the result of a preponderance of feminine virtue being exercised under circumstances that demand the masculine approach. The blame, if there were any advantage to placing it anywhere, is upon the men. The women are not usurping the places of the men, nor would denying them that questionable privilege solve anything. Wives and mothers are being forced to take over the throne from which the husband and father has abdicated. The man has become inoperative.

Where it is the function of the woman to be heart and

center of the family, it is the function of the man to relate his family to the rest of society for the mutual benefit of all. This relating of the family to the community is the root foundation of the married man's vocation. This is his field, his domain. If the man does not control this field then the woman must, and the result will be a disregard for the common good and an over-emphatic concern for the well-being of the individual family. Since the well-being of the individual family should proceed from the common good and not merely be a sum total of all the individual goods, an overconcern for the individual family's welfare will bring about a state of affairs spelling chaos for the whole society. There is a normal tension between the man and wife in regard to the question of the common good. It is the kind of tension that makes for balance. The woman will usually place the good of her family first. For her to do so is normal. The man, if he is truly head of the family, realizes that his family's well-being depends upon the common good and thus will make the common good the first end of his work. With him, that sense called "social consciousness" will not be merely a part-time hobby, but the motivating force in everything he does. When called upon to do so, he will even jeopardize his family's welfare in order to serve the common good. Men have always done this in time of war. It may sometimes be asked of them in time of peace. Today, faced as we are with the need for reorganizing the social order, this responsibility to serve the common good cannot be shirked if we are to avoid complete disaster.

As it was of St. Joseph, the greatest praise for a man is that he be a "just man." The masculine temperament, being objective, logical and direct, is a fitting occasion for the virtue of justice. This is the virtue most lacking in persons and their affairs today. We have evidence of charity, goodwill, emotional sympathy on the part of many people, all of which fail to compensate for the lack of justice. It is typically feminine to be sympathetic for the lot of the impoverished. It is typically masculine to crusade against the injustices which are the root causes of the deprivation.

Matriarchy

The average American family is approaching a matriarchy. Sons are adopting the virtues of their mothers for lack of a substantial display of masculine virtue by the fathers. The movies, radio and comic strips have all adopted this theme of masculine inferiority in the home, and it rings appallingly true to life. Among the faithful in the Church, it is as evident as elsewhere. The expression of the Faith today is primarily private devotion and not public apostolicity, and it is the former that appeals most to women and the latter which appeals most to men. Even the parochial men's groups have taken on a feminine flavor, hardly relieved by an occasional "Sport Nite." Not the least misfortune that results from this feminization is that these male parochial groups act as buffers between the clergy and other men who, though possibly less pious, possess an aggressive masculinity ripe for conversion to the apostolate.

The constant and endless regard of today's good husband for the well-being of his family, so that he saves from the time of their birth for the education of his children, while his neighbor's children starve, or while his local political system grows corrupt, or his Faith goes unchampioned, or his brother is exploited, is a sign of the times. It is goodness measured by the standard of the wife, and thus she is the actual head of the family. This is not good headship measured by any objective standard. Such a father may leave an inheritance of wealth to his sons, whereas what they need most is masculine virtue lived out for their emulation. The son in such a matriarchy of predominately feminine concerns, becomes one of those lads whose lack of masculine virtue has been called "momism." Under stress he becomes inoperative for lack of the soothing hand of a tender woman on his brow. He is of little use to the army, and is poor material for Catholic Action. Unless he mend his ways, the son of such a father will prove to be a greater handicap to his future wife than was his dad. He will be just another child for his wife to care for. Until men go back to the masculine pursuits of devotion to the common good, relating the talents of their children to that end, they will fail to fulfill amply the office of head of the family.

The Causes

The cause of a lapsed fatherhood is not difficult to find. I think there are two root causes. The first is immodesty on the part of women and incontinence on the part of men. The second is intellectual irresponsibility bred by modern methods of work.

Modesty and continence go hand-in-hand. Without either or both virtues men become the slaves of women. The natural tendencies to sexual promiscuity and feminine coquettishness as consequence of original sin, have been aided and intensified by the popular use of contraceptives. Previous to their widespread distribution, male continence was encouraged by women if not by the moral law, for fear of the social tragedy of bearing illegitimate children. Nature, permitted to take its course, rendered a punishment that few women would dare risk incurring. Thus for reasons of respectability as well as morality, certain social precautions were taken to save men from themselves. The most effective of these was modesty in dress. Another was the custom of chaperons, both good Christian customs. The manufacture of contraceptives (made possible by mass-production methods) changed all this. There was nothing to fear now but God (which is ironic, because if God were genuinely feared, neither contraceptives nor mass-production would ever have come into existence!). Women set out to be attractive, and men gave up trying to be continent. The whole social attitude toward woman changed so that today a pious virgin can dress to the point of being indistinguishable from a harlot without evoking any comment more adverse than a whistle.

This change in the character of womanhood drastically revised the common attitude toward marriage. Having children became arbitrary. The female instrument of contraception placed the decision for having children on the shoulders of the mother. It became her prerogative to say how few children she should have. When you add this fact to the obsolescence of the male virtue of continence, it is no wonder that the modern male has become subservient. We would be astonished to discover how many kept women decide the policies of our nation, due to the judicious use of their wiles and the extreme vulnerability of incontinent men.

Wherever the Catholic family continues to maintain the Christian principles of morality in relation to the marriage act, it has to be done unaided by social customs and habits of the same order. Although a wife may be of good will, she may still subscribe to the current social views on female decorum wherever they do not obviously clash with morality. She may still feel that children are arbitrary and encourage the practice of Catholic (?) birth control indiscriminately and for motives hardly sufficient to warrant so dangerous a practice. The man may consider his wife an exception while continuing to hold the current views toward womanhood.

This will not only try his fidelity, but also make him unfit to guide his growing sons and daughters. Private virtue in regard to chastity will always be seriously threatened until it is accompanied by public customs of morality.

The second cause of the loss of male headship may very well be a remote consequence of the first. It is otherwise difficult to explain why men have for so long tolerated a social system so detrimental to the fulfillment of their vocations. The concentration of productive property in the hands of a few has left the average husband no alternative but to let himself out for hire. He no longer possesses either the skills, the property, or the tools to set his own motives or standard of work. Returning home from an office where all his conquests have been of doubtful merit to the community at large, or from a factory where his efficiency is measured by mechanical standards, he can maintain dominion over his family only by reversing the habits which have characterized his day. What virtues he does possess can only be revealed to his children under home circumstances much more favorable to his wife. He finds himself helping her in tasks of her own invention, doing work which she initiates. In the eyes of the children and his wife, he soon assumes a subordinate role. It is small wonder that the suburban husband, in more cases than one, seems somewhat less formidably masculine than his wife!

To Reassure the Ladies

A casual glance at the foregoing arguments might lead my lady readers to arm themselves against a turbulent and bloody revolution espoused by the menfolk. Housewives might run to the dry goods store for scarlet draping material to match the color of the blood soon to be shed in their living rooms. Dear old dad, they may suspect, will go about like some Charles Laughtonesque lion seeking whom he may devour. Becoming once again the head of the family might go to father's head. By contrast, with the new regime, the Barretts of Wimpole Street will be considered a family with a hen-pecked father. For that reason, before jumping to such conclusions (or, if you will, arriving at intuitive perceptions), I hope that the ladies' glances will be more than casual. Whatever a male headship may add to a household will be something more satisfying than bruises or broken heads. It might be that peace of mind so vainly sought by neurotic matrons in the book of that same name. At any rate it will be a state of affairs which a more sane people than we considered normal.

Whatever the specific remedy may be, the general prescription is this. Men must return to the concept of manhood in which each man is considered to have a mission to fulfill. This mission is related to first, the honor and glory of God; second, the common good, and third, to his specific contribution to each. In the work of fulfilling this mission, some men take a helpmate so that in one flesh and one mind and one heart, they may more effectively accomplish this mission. As a result of this holy union, children are born. These children, in turn, are educated by word and deed to a physical, intellectual and spiritual maturity so that they, too, may take up the mission to which God has called them. As you can also see that it calls for a kind of apostolicity, and more than that, a conversion. Without this Christian concept the family has only half a meaning, and that is the woman's half. When only this half-meaning is known the children are all dressed up with no place to go. They are prepared, but no one knows for what. Everyone is getting ready for a great occasion which never happens. The meaning that the man gives to the family is purpose, direction, motive and end.

When groups of families get together to discuss these things, Christ will be there in the midst of them, and so, too, Mary and Joseph. The job of the men will be to discover what their specific missions are. The job of the women will be to discover how they can best assist their husbands in the accomplishment of their missions. As time goes on with corporate discussion and personal meditation, the men will see, as their Holy Father has, that their vocations must be part of the Church's crusade to restore the affairs of men to Christ. This will become the end which gives meaning to their every act. What was first an evening spent in companionable and neighborly discussion, will become for them a new way of life. As they look back on their lives they will see as its milestones, not their first pair of long pants, or their school graduation, or the first dollar they earned, or the first time they met their wives, but rather they will see those magnificent steps to maturity in Christ, baptism, penance, the Eucharist and matrimony.

The work which fills the days of these men will fall under greater scrutiny. They will reform it to coincide with the laws of charity and justice courageously without fear of consequence, knowing how ridiculous and imprudent it is to seek security elsewhere than in the furtherance of God's Will. They may conclude that the work they are now doing is without merit and directed solely toward the profit of the owners at the expense of the common good. Then they will consider ways and means to abstract themselves from that job, so that they may better use the talents that God has given them for His purpose.

These are the things that men can do to regain the headship of the family. You may wonder that I have said little about religious practices or the cultivation of virtue.

Can it be that I am putting too much emphasis on the social problem and not enough on the problems of the spirit? That is not my intention. Once men have become aware of the magnificent mission to which they have been called, they will hunger for the Eucharist as they have never hungered before. Their virtue will not be cultivated merely by quiet spiritual exercises, but rather come as the consequence of Christ acting through them in their daily apostolate. With a new purposefulness, the new Christian man will lift his fellows from the quiet desperation of their lives, and in acting Christ-like, he will be setting for his children an example which is the crowning glory of fatherhood.

THE FATHER IN THE HOME

Ed Willock

**The man's view of the making of the home is
different from the woman's. That is not because it is
contradictory but because it is complementary.
The solution to irresponsible fatherhood is not
to be found along the lines of feminine standards
of "good behavior."**

In order to approach this article I had to put aside two
misgivings concerning the subject. The first and most obvious drawback is my realization of some of my own deficien-
cies as a father. The second misgiving is that I would have
preferred to write an article more properly entitled "The
Father's Place Is Not in the Home." I'd find this subject more
to my taste because I feel strongly that an erroneous conscience is trying to domesticate modern fathers whereas, in
fact, their proper environment is in the wilderness of politics
(in the broad sense), that is, the interfamily area. The fact
that the nineteenth-century father was consistently naughty
whenever he was away from home is no reason for conclud-
ing that it would improve his demeanor to make him a
mother's helper. Maybe a man is better for being under a
woman's guiding eye, but at best he could only be a better
son. The father's job pertains primarily, I think, to the social

order and secondarily to the domestic order. To fit these convictions into the subject I have been appointed to treat however, only means that I must talk about the other side of a question which fortunately has two sides. The father undoubtedly has a job to do in the home.

No Mother's Helper

It might seem that I am being negative to begin my definition of domestic fatherhood with an insistence upon what it is *not*. However, the situation as it exists is indeed a negative one. So called *spiritually-minded* people are currently implying that bad men should become good boys. That is to say, religious people who (for good reason) stand aghast at the irresponsible behavior of today's fathers, seem to think that to reform the situation means that men should capitulate to feminine standards of good behavior. This I consider extremely negative. A reformed father is not a good boy. If he were a good boy he would do what his wife expects of him. As a good man, however, it should be expected that he would often do the unexpected. The father must be the head of the house, and that means if and when he becomes a better man it will be in accordance with his own idea of perfection and not his wife's. To say other than this is to imply that mother knows best. If she knows best, then God would have made her the head of the house. He didn't.

For the past quarter century Catholicism as parochially practiced in this country has had two remarkable and somewhat diametrical characteristics. The majority opinion which prevailed in the pulpit and at the dinner table was (and is) that feminine prudence (valuable in its proper place) corresponds most perfectly with Christian behavior. Virtue always seemed to lie on the side of stability, domesticity, gentleness, sympathy, obedience, and a cautious concern for one's own family. All of this corresponded very nicely with the mother's inclinations as well as the fulfillment of her vocation.

The minority opinion, generally voiced by the father and possibly the grown-up children, concerned itself more with freedom, revolution, justice, social consciousness, skepticism, and the need for risking one's good to gain a greater good. This opinion labored under the handicap that it was unorthodox, unconventional, and seemed to coincide with the views of people who were obviously no-good. The fact that it corresponded in many details with the expressed views of the Papacy was not generally known.

If during this same quarter century the destiny of Catholic families had been guided by the fathers, things might have been different, but the facts are that secular mores also concurred regarding the primacy of feminine prudence. Everything conspired to increase the prestige of domesticity and feminine counsel, including the irresponsibility of fathers and silence in regard to Papal direction.

The frustration of this minority opinion has produced an abortive rebelliousness characterized by aberrations that run the gamut all the way from wanton alcoholism to fastidious pacifism. The more drunk or the more pacific the rebels have become, the more convinced are those who hold the majority view that they are right. Consequently, current attempts to Christianize father are too often a re-intensification of the attempt to domesticate the man, that is, to make him the helpmate of the woman in her task of running the home.

I wish to have no part in this re-domestication of the male animal, so when I write about the father in the home I am writing about the man exercising his God-given discretion as head of the house in company with his beloved helpmate, and his masculine contribution to the formation of the children. This may or may not coincide with his wife's conviction as to how he should act.

Every father must learn to use his own head and respect the opinions of his wife. Yet his must be the decision in a situation for which there is no formula.

The Children's Hour

For most men, today, the evening meal is the time of closest contact with their families. It may be well to prolong this meal so that more can be made of the opportunity. The father should give the blessing, asking thanks of God. Young children should be discouraged from talking or from occupying the stage so completely that the adults, father, mother and guests, cannot talk seriously and sociably. It should be borne in mind that this conversation concerning adult matters is mainly for the benefit of the children and a contribution to their education. This would be the sole limitation that could generally be placed upon adult conversation in the presence of children: that the matter and demeanor are toward their edification.

The good of the children should be placed first, and adults should not indulge too often in their normal desire to get away from the youngsters. I think it's a good idea to have guests frequently, eating dinner with the children present because during this time of conversation the visitor can be drawn out to express ideas informative and edifying to the children. These evening meals are the most likely time for increasing the social scope of the children. They emerge temporarily from their childhood world to gaze curiously at the vocational adult world. The meal, joined in by all, breaks down the normal barriers between childhood and grown-up matters. During these few minutes the child is more susceptible to persuasion than throughout his schoolday.

Any and all matters should be considered fit topics for conversation as long as a certain guidance is maintained in the direction of idealism. I differ with those who hold that spiritual reading is to be preferred to conversation. This is just one of the innumerable attempts to convert family living in accordance with monastic norms. It must be borne in mind that the family vocation is concerned above all with *the proper use of creatures* whereas monastic living concerns itself with *utmost detachment from creatures.* The great achievement in a family is not to produce many priests and nuns but to pave the way toward the vocation which God wishes the child to accept. Whatever calling seems to be attractive to the child is fit matter for family conversation, *including* aspirations to the convent or priesthood. I act upon the assumption that a respect for any holy vocation from farming to the priesthood is the proper disposition for discovering one's own vocation. It is foolish to intimate that to cultivate in the children a respect for created things—music, nature, painting, child raising, politics or plumbing—distracts the child's attention from eternal concerns. This intimation springs from a conviction even more erroneous: that holy people *scorn* creation.

The father as head of the family should guide the progress of conversation at meals. His presence and demeanor at the meal has a profound effect on the children. He must either use it wisely or abuse it. There is no third alternative.

Some fathers have found it wise to conclude the evening meal with family prayers. It might be easier to do this than to reassemble the family later. Another advantage in doing this is that there is less likelihood that the prayers will be inordinately prolonged. In regard to family prayers there are a few generalizations that can be made. These prayers are the family conversation with God and His saints. It should be taken for granted that every home will converse in its own unique way. Once the children know by heart the formal petitions recommended by the Church, then it is wise to introduce as many spontaneous innovations as are required to hold the attention of the children. A marathon of rosaries, reducing prayer to the level of a mere feat of endurance, can generate a distaste for prayer, and more than this give prayer an entirely false significance. Austerity is one thing and prayer is another. Praying can be joyful and it can be a bore. I think that for children it should be made as dramatic and joyful as possible. A little imagination on the part of the parents accomplishes much more than a mere dogged determination to see how many times they can (spiritually speaking) chin themselves.

Recreation

In discussing this topic I must depend a good deal upon generalities. The running of a home is an art, not a science. What works in one home does not work in another. If I use generalities, then I am not being purposefully vague but conscientiously liberal.

In most American homes today, after the evening meal is over, there are still chores remaining for the wife to do, whereas the husband's time is at his own discretion. This situation produces natural tensions that should be expected. It is reasonable to assume that a wife dislikes plunging herself into dishwater while Daddy adjourns to his evening paper. Something should be said for Daddy in this instance, however. In general, wage-earners and tradesmen work at a far more vigorous pace than housewives. Most men who work on production for their income are delighted to find two or three minutes in the workday which they can call their own.

Housewives, because they are their own bosses, and because they work in co-operation with nature, generally work at a slower pace than wage-earners meeting machine demands. Although this is fraught with all kinds of exceptions, it is generally true that the wage-earner is more in need of a rest after supper than the housewife. The significant point is that the time of recreation for the husband seldom coincides with the time of recreation for his wife.

The Man's Task

According to the custom of judging a husband's virtue entirely by his behavior *when he concludes his work,* his day's toil is disregarded and he is considered a heel if he doesn't wash the dishes or help put the children to bed, yet there is never any question of his wife helping with his daily toil. At times a husband should help his wife with domestic tasks, but it should be taken for granted that these are not *his* tasks, but hers.

This brings us back to the obvious question, "What is the man's task in the home?" Keeping in mind my previously expressed opinion that a husband's work is not primarily in the home, and remembering the fact that his conduct at home follows after his daily stint, we must probe fairly deep to find out just what his domestic role really is. Most of the arguments from the nature of the sexes are rather weak. For example, I doubt if there is anything in the feminine temperament which prescribes that she wash dishes, nor is there anything in the masculine make-up which gives him supremacy at the art of repairing electric-light cords. Tradition is more helpful. The domestic jobs must be divided, and customarily certain groups of tasks fit together for the wife and others for the husband. These are by no means absolute designations. No man will become effeminate from washing dishes now and then, nor will repairing an electric-light cord cause a wife to grow a beard.

The least vague principle governing masculine and feminine tasks in the home, that I can think of, is that the wife cares for current and immediate needs and the man takes care of the long-range destiny of the home. Whereas it is normal for her to answer in response to each call that arises, it is normal for him to exercise foresight and plan for the future. The woman will cope with many crises whereas his job is to foresee and avert catastrophe. The cross of the wife is that she will have to adjust herself to observing her husband engaged in long-range ventures, such as repairing a roof that doesn't yet leak, planning or building a home, taking part in organizational activities, while (in her mind) current problems are left unattended. The cross of the husband is that he must realize that averting catastrophe is seldom appreciated as much as coping with catastrophe (that is why young boys aspire to be firemen rather than carpenters).

Helpmates

My anti-feminist leanings should not be construed as a lack of respect for the personal dignity of the wife and mother. Quite the contrary. When men once again become heads of their home, the dignity of wifeliness and motherhood will equal if not surpass the current secular adulation of the career woman. In the evening after the children are bedded is the most likely time for the man and wife to sit together and talk about their mutual partnership. A few words may be all that is needed to renew common enthusiasm for the daily grind. When God divided the species into two and assigned the woman to be the helpmate of the man, He didn't merely give the man an extra pair of hands but another mind and loving heart. It is more than likely that a man and wife can get better advice on intimate problems of conduct *from one*

another than from any other source. Grace and love combine to quicken the perceptions of each partner so they can
be of inestimable help to one another. It should be borne in
mind that all the graces of Matrimony build upon the mutual consent of each partner. Each had to say, "I will" before
the Sacrament was fulfilled, and this "I will!" must be repeated continuously if the graces are to become actual in
their works. In order for the man to be a proper head of the
family, his wife must continuously consent to it. He cannot
effectively force her to consent. On the other hand, the man
must consent to her being his helper or else she cannot truly
be helpful. If he seeks advice for living from some other
sources, looking down upon her suggestions, then he is cut-
ting himself off from the most likely source of wisdom.

Other Matters

There are innumerable matters that are part of family
living which I have not touched upon. There is no formula
for doing the right thing at the right time either in the Church
or outside it. Civilized living has done much to lessen the
differences in gifts between men and women, and differences that are extremely obvious (and taken for granted) in a
peasant society, are quite subtle and almost hidden in urban
living. It is an over-simplification to assume that primitive
living is the true measure of what is right in domestic relations. The relationship between man and wife is dynamic
and subject to all sorts of unpredictable changes. Both partners must learn to adapt themselves gracefully to the changing pattern, much as two dancing partners respond to the
changing tempo of the music.

It is sometimes assumed, for example, that financial
matters are properly the man's domain. If so, I can't imagine
why. The education of the children is another thing assigned

one way or the other. Here again, the only safe generaliza-
tion is that financial and educational matters fall at one time
to the woman and another time to the man, depending upon
whether immediate or long-range objectives are involved.
Women do seem to have a greater capacity for response to
immediate, personal needs. Men do seem to have a greater
capacity for speculation and foresight. Obviously both gifts
are very necessary to the proper conduct of a family. It seems
fairly reasonable that the woman should endeavor to pass on
her gifts to the girls and the man pass on his to the boys.

Special Concern Today

In another age men would have a more pronounced domestic role than they have today. We are living in an age of
great change. Among those contending for influence in establishing a new pattern for living to replace the hectic era
that is passing, is the Catholic Church. The Church has called
for a marked reintegration of persons and institutions bringing them into harmony with the mission of Christ. We, as
Catholics, therefore cannot presume upon a *business as usual*
policy, especially not in our homes. We are retooling the
home for Christian living.

Since foresight is the special prerogative of the father, he
is the one most responsible to bring these changes about.
Usually his job, from whence he gains income, has nothing
whatever to do with this responsibility to bring about change.
Thus his spare time often becomes the only period of time
when he is free to establish a new order. It is a time for study,
conference, organization, and apostolic works, directed toward this end of revolution. Most Catholic men do very
little in this regard, tossing an even greater burden upon
those who feel responsible. Consequently, one finds in many
homes fathers wasting their time at childish games for fear

or ignorance about how to face properly their paternal responsibilities in a changing world. In fewer homes one finds fathers rushing about to the apparent neglect of immediate tasks, trying to organize and agitate for revolution. Most men do too little, a few men do too much. All Catholic men should respond to the universal call for Catholic Action.

The good of every family depends upon the father's active participation in this common goal of reordering society. The few who try to do the work of many appear to be fools, often to their wives. Other men attend simply to the immediate needs of their own families, thus winning feminine favor, yet jeopardizing by their negligence the very institution of the family itself.

Close to the Church

It is vitally important that the Catholic father realize that many of his vocational convictions coincide nicely with the precepts of Peter even though they might not at all agree with the business as usual, conservative attitude which characterizes American parochial life. He should put himself in contact with the tradition of St. Joseph and St. Peter, and familiarize himself with the paternal prudence which is so integral a part of the Church. Few fathers realize their own dignity as fathers, and few see the unique role that the Church insists they play in this work of revolutionary change. He should recognize that the American tradition of the last quarter century, which assigns to him the role of eternal adolescence, is a belittlement of his vocation. He is the bridge between Church and state. He is the bridge between state and family. He is the bridge between family and Church. If this is not clear to us today, at least it should be obvious that all these bridges are down.

THE ECONOMICS OF THE CATHOLIC FAMILY

Walter John Marx

Any talk of the economics of the big Catholic family
will always come to the problem of providing for
additional babies and aged parents. Modern suburbia
is often an occasion to sin against duty in these areas.
Radical analysis of how to insure a stable and
vigorous Catholic population points to a rural
environment.

In the early spring of 1948, a national conference on
family life was held in Washington. Depending upon each
speaker's particular background and religious and social be-
liefs, there was much disagreement over the path that should
be taken to strengthen the family as the key unit of society.
With some exceptions, however, there was general agreement
that things were not entirely well with the American family.
The rising tide of juvenile delinquency furnished evidence
hard to refute on this point. But at the conference, and later,
many of the reforms suggested ran counter both to our demo-
cratic traditions and to the teachings of the Church regarding the role of the family in society.

Perhaps the most dangerous trend of our times in this

respect is to emphasize remedies which, in fact if not in theory, hasten the disintegration of the family. There appears to be a general distrust of parents by the sociologists, psychologists, and social workers. For example, the United States Commissioner of Education at the end of the school term in 1948 suggested that the long summer vacation be abolished for school children on the theory that it was better to have the children under school supervision than under that of their parents. Organized play and after-school activities, designed to keep idle hands busy, do withdraw the children from an additional segment of family life until the home becomes a combination dormitory and light-lunch establishment. Family activities appear to have little place in the planning of those professional planners concerned with the problems of modern youth.

I have no intention here of repeating once more the general Catholic stand regarding the family. As a one-time professor of history I can say that I know of no civilization that has long endured without a vigorous family life. One of the early marks of the disintegration of a civilization is the decay of family life, a decline in marriages, an increase in divorces and a refusal to have children. Most Catholics give at least lip service to the Catholic ideal of the family, although the decline in the Catholic birth rate, as the Catholic family moves upward in the economic bracket, leads one to suspect that in actual practice, Catholics are often little better than their neighbors.

Without attempting to defend Catholics who give in to the ways of the world, I should like to discuss at some length the economic factors affecting the observance by Catholics of the Church's teaching regarding the family. For the sake of clarity and because of the limitations of space, I may have to oversimplify somewhat the problem and the solution. The reader, however, will have no trouble in filling in the qualifications and the elaborations which should go with the discussion.

We all know the purpose of Christian marriage. The matter is discussed frequently from the pulpit and in the Catholic press. However, let us take a typical case and see just what happens to a young Catholic couple attempting to carry out the teachings of the Church in a materialistic world ruled largely by the "iron laws" of economics. Before marriage, Joe and Mary had many discussions regarding the economic base of their marriage. Joe, being a young man, was not making a great deal of money. Perhaps Mary had a stenographer's job and it was decided that both would keep on working until the first baby arrived, or until they had an apartment or a small home furnished. Being an average young couple they could not hope to buy their own place.

The first year of marriage was not too difficult. In view of the housing shortage, they were quite happy in finding a one-room efficiency apartment. Their wedding presents and their combined incomes enabled them to furnish their small place rather nicely. Their first real economic problem came with the arrive of the baby. In spite of their combined incomes, they somehow had not been able to save up sufficient money to pay for the hospital and doctor bills. Joe had taken out hospital insurance, but the baby arrived before he could use the insurance for the hospital bill. Then there were the many expenses he had not thought about, a crib, diapers, a sudden surge in the laundry bill, periodic doctor bills for monthly checkups of the baby, bottles, a sterilizer, *etc.* Later came prepared baby foods, a baby carriage, clothes, *etc.* And now the family was forced to live on a single salary. The one-room apartment became impossible. Besides, the landlord gave them an eviction notice because children were not allowed in his apartment house and the baby annoyed the neighbors. Then came the dreary search for a larger apartment in a building tolerating children. Because of the expenses caused by the baby, it was necessary to get a larger place for a rental no higher and preferably lower than the first place. Incredible though it seems, Joe and Mary did find such an apartment, but in a shabbier section of town. They were unable to buy any additional furniture but at least they had a place for the baby's crib.

The cost of the second baby was not so high. Hospital insurance took care of most of the hospital bill, although the hospital authorities found some thirty dollars that was not covered by insurance. Many of the things purchased for the first baby could be used for the second baby. They did have to buy another crib and their daily cost of living mounted as they took care of two babies. They sold the old car Joe had before his marriage and they found it more and more difficult to buy clothes for themselves. Because of the cost of the diaper service, Mary now began to wash her own diapers.

Joe received a modest raise in pay the third year, but this did not equal the rise in the cost of living index and took no account of his increasing family responsibilities. I won't go on and describe the later history of Joe and Mary. Inexorably, each additional baby meant for them a lowering of their standard of living, a further push toward the slum. As the children grew, there were shoes to buy, the food bill went up, clothes became an increasing expense. School proved to be an additional burden. Worst of all, from the point of view of the parents, their children were being raised in an unhealthy environment of city streets and parking lots, whizzing autos, idle playmates with temptations and false values on all sides. Except for the mysterious workings of God's providence, which somehow enables families such as Joe and

Mary's to survive, one does not see why their family should not eventually disintegrate into the hands of the welfare agencies as the economic burden becomes insupportable.

In its advocacy of family allowances, the Church has an answer for part of the problem presented above. However, the most generous family allowance yet voted by any government, cannot begin to equal the actual cost of raising a child. The environmental factors mentioned above remain even with a family allowance. A recent survey indicated that of church members in the United States, the Baptists and the Catholics were the poorest. We know that we Catholics are concentrated particularly in the great Eastern cities. Monsignor Ligutti, O.E. Baker and others have drummed into us over and over again the undeniable fact that our great cities cannot reproduce themselves. This means that the Catholic Church in America, anchored in the big cities, is faced ultimately with a declining membership unless sufficient converts can be made to counteract the declining birth rate of the cities. Because of the factors noted above, we cannot assume that Catholic urban families will reverse the normal urban trend. The history of the Catholics in Quebec who have moved to the cities demonstrates this fact.

When, then, is to be done? Obviously, one of the first things is to attempt to change the environment of the family to one more favorable for family health and well-being. Urbanism ultimately means death for the family. Each additional child means a lowering of the family's standard of living and the necessity of finding larger housing quarters.

Instead of starting off in a city apartment, Mary and Joe could have purchased an acre or two of land in the country within commuting distance of Joe's job. In order to get a home for themselves, they could have lived in even a prefabricated garage and done without modern improvements until they could pay for them out of the money they would otherwise have spent for rent. Perhaps their families, on weekends, could help them build at least a cinder-block or frame shell in which they could live while finishing it off. Or perhaps parish guilds or young men's organizations could, in a weekend or two, throw up a shell much in the spirit of the old house-raisings in colonial America. A garden, a couple of goats or a cow, and perhaps a pig or two and a few chickens would, in the long run, be more profitable to the family than Mary's job in the city, and as the children arrived, the extra food cost would not be so apparent. At a surprisingly early age, the children could begin to share in the responsibility of providing food for the family by taking care of some of the livestock.

In place of the crowded city environment, the children would grow up in the open air with plenty of play space. By choosing the cheaper land, well off a busy highway, money is saved and the children kept from an untimely death from a passing auto or truck. I know one man with a larger place who, with the birth of every son, plants a sufficient number of trees on his place to grow up into marketable lumber by the time his son is ready for college so that his expenses will be paid. With one more child eating eggs, it is no great burden to the family to add a hen or two to the laying flock.

With food and shelter taken care of, most of the battle is won. A home-built house can easily be expanded to take care of new little residents. In my own case, for example, now that our fifth baby has arrived, I am preparing to change the shed roof of part of our structure to a gable roof giving me space for a room upstairs. My oldest boy, five at the end of October, is the owner of a seven-month old milk goat and is already being trained in its care and management. Little Lois, a year younger, helps us feed the chickens every day and even little Anton, who is just three, helps his mother bring in the laundry from the line.

When youngsters reach their teens in the city, they are still heavy and, indeed, increasing burdens upon their families. In the country, by that time, they are already more than paying their own way through the aid given in developing the various home enterprises. Their work teaches them self-reliance, responsibility and resourcefulness. They learn there is no magical way to get the things they need and want without working for them.

I am restricting myself to a discussion of the economic basis of the family, but the reader will easily realize that there are even more important considerations involved in the sort of family I am describing, the additional strength of a family in which each member takes some part in the family enterprise, the family planning involved in which the children are encouraged to take a part, the health that comes from outdoor living and exercise, the constant evidence of God's work when one labors with growing things, the skills that are acquired easily and naturally. Every one of my boys, by the time he is seventeen, will have a rough mastery of the carpenter's, mason's, plumber's and electrician's trades, in addition to the ability to grow things in the soil. He will be able to build his own home with his own hands and in the precarious times ahead will have the versatile background necessary for survival. My girls will have similar training along lines complementing the activities of the boys.

In discussing the economics of the Christian family, I have emphasized the problem of providing for additional babies. But the older folks, too, form part of a family, and one of the many tragedies of our times is the inability of the average family to take over the support of aged parents who, at times, have impoverished themselves in order to give the

children a "good start." The city apartment obviously was
not designed for the care of one's parents or in-laws. Even if
a large enough apartment could be found and paid for, the
nervous tension of so many people living so closely together
is often too great. Here again, the rural home provides a
solution. Additional quarters with extra privacy can be erected
at nominal cost. The old man who always seems in the way
in an apartment, becomes largely self-sustaining with a garden and a few chickens of his own. He becomes the playmate and the arbiter of his grandchildren. He has new self-
respect as he feels that he is pulling his own weight in the
family's economy.

For the reasons noted above, an increasing number of
families, Catholic and non-Catholic, are deserting the cities
for rural environments even when it is necessary in most
cases to retain a city job. Few families regret the move although it is absolutely necessary that both husband and wife
agree upon the wisdom of making the change before taking
the final step. It is helpful also if two or more families with
similar ideas settle near enough to each other to permit the
women to visit and compare notes. The isolated family can
succeed only in the event the woman is remarkably self-suf-
ficient and does not mind the loneliness of a rather secluded
life. It is not my purpose in this article to discuss the spiritual and moral development that would be possible in a whole
community of such families with its own school and church.

I do not wish to minimize the importance of the family-
allowance plan. In our present society some such plan is essential, but the money would render more effective help to
the large family if the family were in a rural environment
where the subsidiary members of the family could produce
real wealth at home. The production by the family of as
many of its own needs as possible seems to be the only way

in which a young couple can bear and rear children in a healthy environment, frugal no doubt, without many modern conveniences, but receiving the essentials of adequate and healthy shelter and good food.

I speak from personal experience. I have heard so many city youngsters plead for the glass of milk their mother did not have, or for the second helping at the table that could not be given. No matter how desperate our situation, so long as we have our land and our cow, my tiny tots have all the rich raw milk thy can drink, with none of the vitamins pasteurized out. When the cow goes dry next summer, we expect our two milk goats to come into production. In the meantime, our cow provides also our butter and milk for the neighbor's children until their own goats come in fresh. My children are outdoors from dawn until dark. They have excellent appetites and go to sleep promptly in the evening after their prayers. Before we moved to the country, they were pale and anemic, dawdled over their food and refused to go to sleep without repeated spankings. They copy my efforts in the garden with dime tools I bought for them. They attempt to help me in my building operations and next year I shall buy the oldest some simple carpenter tools. They pick wild berries in season, watch the chickens or play with the goats and the cats. In the evening they will be waiting to meet me, perhaps part way down the gravel road to my place so that they can ride a short distance with me, all talking at once, reciting the day's events and trying to enlist my help in any number of their private enterprises. We have our winter's potatoes from our garden, a laying flock of chickens that supplies us with fresh eggs, and enough of a surplus to pay for the feed and we have made a start at least on growing our own feed. The size of our family means that there are always hand-me-down clothes for the younger ones to wear. Surplus bunk beds from the army solve the sleeping problem. Next year I shall plant a little more food to take care of little Eric who arrived last summer. Attractively-printed feed sacks make clothes for the younger children. I have not yet licked the shoe problem, a very real one with baby shoes at five dollars a pair, but if things got desperate, I would insist on reverting to my boyhood in northern Alaska and make Eskimo-type footgear out of the skins of our own animals.

There are so many advantages to this way of living that I find it difficult to restrict myself to a discussion solely of its economics. There are so many intangible psychological factors involved, the element of stability, the feeling of security which children have when living in a house of their own, surrounded by land that they can never get in a city apartment. Most Europeans look upon America as a matriarchal society since the man seems to exist merely to bring home a salary check. What training the children get outside of school comes primarily from the mother. In the above plan of living, in the evening and on weekends the father is in intimate contact with his children and can assume some of the responsibility for their training. They help in simple tasks, run errands, get a tool I lack for a particular job, and so forth. Even in heavy tasks where my full strength just barely succeeds in balancing some heavy object, the extra push of my two small boys creates the necessary margin for success. Nicky watches me milk the cow every evening and when his hands are a little larger, that is a chore he will take over. There is also a wonderful feeling about being one's own master in the country. My children can make as much noise as they wish. If I want to keep a pig or two, I need ask no man's consent. I have my own water supply, I could get my own fuel from my woods. There are fish, crabs and oysters just off my property and the only reason I have not enjoyed them so far is that I have spent my spare time in building and cultivating. In two or three years the boys will enjoy fishing and crabbing and will be able to satisfy their mother's love of sea food.

As I have mentioned above, God's providence is the only explanation we can give for the success of so many large families raised under incredible difficulties in urban slums. But we should take advantage of the natural means God has given us in order to make easier the raising of a Christian family. We can increase in sanctity by resisting our daily temptations. At the same time we are taught not to expose ourselves wilfully to occasions of sin. For many people the city is just such an occasion of sin. The economic pressure alone leads to birth control, if not to outright thievery and embezzlement. The problem is critical for the Church in America and it will be necessary to multiply the efforts of the National Catholic Rural Life Conference many times if we are to insure a stable and vigorous Catholic population in the next century, or, dare I say, in the next depression when the abject dependence of the urban population will at once become apparent.

AFRAID TO MARRY?

Ed Willock

Raising children is the primary social act. There is no vocation more essential to the reorganizing of the social order than fatherhood. Catholic fatherhood is a strenuous job requiring courage, aggressiveness, and sacrifice. The selfish man is not fit for marriage and a woman should steer clear of him.

I have always contended that one with minor talents should be content to play a minor role. That is why I make no attempt here to be profound but only to be provocative. This slice of prose is designed not to solve a difficulty but to start an argument.

When I state (as I do) that the evils of individualism are being perpetuated above all by our unmarried men, I don't expect such a charge to solve anything—but I am wistfully hopeful that it will start something. Nor do I apologize for so sweeping a generality merely because there are exceptions. When we deal with things *as they are,* such sweeping generalities are as close as one can hope to come to the truth. It would be very convenient for the critics of society if there were some dogma or formulae that applied to social mores. Fortunately there are not. I cannot say that all unmarried men are irresponsible. I charge no young man of my acquaintance with selfishness. I merely contend that the generality of single men are afraid to marry, so afraid, in fact, that there are some eight million over the age of thirty in this country who have avoided its burdens altogether.

I had occasion, a few years back, to address a series of talks to groups of engaged young men. I frequently noted (aloud) that the advanced years and demeanor of my audience was such as to lead one to suspect that the Sacrament they immediately anticipated was Extreme Unction rather than Matrimony. Their caution verging on phobia reminded me of a line of Oscar Wilde's: "Seldom had men looked so sadly on the sky!" Whatever enthusiasm they might have had lay hidden behind a grim preoccupation with the direful possibility that babies might be forthcoming.

These prospective grooms had more than the traditional and normal pre-marital jitters. Somehow they sensed that in choosing to marry and have a family they were rashly departing from standard operating procedure. One young man, for example, lifted no eyebrows among his fellows when he attempted to involve me in hypothetical speculations as to whether he should, as a prudent parent, have some assurance of his financial ability to provide a college education for his child-to-be, before setting in motion the chain of circumstances which would make this studious child's existence likely. I rudely refused to become involved, saying that (as far as I could see) worries concerning the advanced education of an unborn child on the part of a yet unwed parent were more indicative of panic than prudence. At that point in the proceedings I made an observation which I will repeat here since it lies at the root of the discussion in which we are involved.

Holy Matrimony

Catholic marriage requires that the couple have a fairly precise notion of what the Sacrament means and the state involves. Facing these facts is frightening after one has become used to the term "marriage" as covering every possible eventuality, including legal cohabitation and the "girl-for-you-a-boy-for-me" clambake. When we start to be definitive and precise in our terminology, realizing that Matrimony implies *sacrifice*, that it holds out the large family as its ideal, that it expects parents to give their lives (and give up their "fun") for their children, then we begin to see that Matrimony is as radical a departure from the ideals of self-satisfaction by which we commonly live as any foreign "ism." The defense of culture, religion, and tradition is essentially a defense of the Sacrament of Matrimony. In practice, Christian marriage generally implies a preference for babies rather than baubles.

In other words, to take Matrimony seriously is to deny almost every postulate upon which our social habits are based. It is to defend fidelity and loyalty, it is to prefer the generation to come to one's own pleasure, it is to prefer an economy which supports the large family rather than the shrewd trader. Many married people have discovered various loopholes (they think) by which then can enjoy the conveniences and pleasures of marriage while closing their eyes to its responsibilities. The prospective novice is not so capable of self-deception, consequently he's scared to death. The sad result of this fear (or one of them) is that the most likely recruit in the papal push to reorganize the social order, the young father, is gradually becoming a rarity.

Social Responsibility

I expect an argument on that point of the "most likely

recruit," so let me explain. The so-called "social" encyclicals have not been enthusiastically received in the United States. Here is one reason for the indifference. The Sacrament most directly concerned with the social area is Matrimony. It brings into being the social unit: the family. Raising children is the primary cultural act. The best measure of the social order is its fitness for children (which is also a good measure of a family, neighborhood or city). To reorganize the social order is a strenuous and difficult task requiring courage and aggressiveness. There is no vocation to which it is more essential than that of fatherhood. Usually only the young father has the energy and zest for such a task. One should not expect priests or monks to be greatly excited about social reform. The priest has his routine pastoral duties, and his preoccupation with the eternal verities and spiritual welfare leaves him little time to bother with political or economic matters. Women generally find fulfillment in personal and domestic matters. Social re-organization is not primarily their meat.

If these facts are true, indifference to the inspired papal directives concerning social change indicates a weakening of the vocation of fatherhood. I am dealing here with one social factor contributing to this weakness, namely, the tendency in young men to flee the marital bonds or else postpone the step to such an age that they are no longer alert or energetic enough to accept the challenges that accompany the vocation.

The Higher State

I realize in bringing this point up that I am touching upon a problem which interests only a minority of Catholic young men. Most single men justify their irresponsibility toward marriage by the generally accepted law of life, namely, "Look out for number one!" I admire their logic. It is only their premise with which I would quarrel.

There is a small group however, many of whom are ex-seminarians, who justify their flight from harness upon a theological point which states that the single state is a *higher* state. This point is but vaguely understood and resembles in profundity the proverbial alibi of the late husband: "I was sitting up with a sick friend." Whatever St. Paul had in mind (for it is to him they vaguely refer), I am sure he was not recommending social irresponsibility. It is apparent that those men (and women) who choose the disciplines of religious obedience and trials of community living to wedded bliss have chosen a more direct route to heaven. It is also apparent that a rare individual can give more selfless service to society by remaining single.

But a young man beholden to no one, answerable only to his own whims (however much he identifies these whims with the movement of the Holy Spirit) has reason to doubt the spiritual altitude at which he is flying. Religious superiors and wives perform a similar function in that they help a man distinguish between whimsy and duty. Without one or the other to keep him in line a young man is likely to wallow in a home-made asceticism or aestheticism which shorn of pious terminology is only a peculiar form of self-indulgence. Apart from the tasks of monks and clergy, there are very few works, corporal or spiritual, that cannot be done as well by the married as the single.

I am not at all reluctant to admit the possibility that there can be exceptions to this generality. God's ways are far too mysterious to be fitted nicely into a sociological pattern no matter how wisely conceived. Yet there is one point the single man should dwell upon when he considers the justifiability of his state before God. He should face the fact that however blithesome he finds his individuality, in choosing it he is inadvertently condemning some girl to the same predicament.

A MAN'S WORK

Elaine Malley

A man's essential task is outside the home. A man is fulfilled and sanctified by work, identifies with Christ's work of redemption, and receives moral and emotional sustenance from his family's love. Men are not substitute mothers. A man's work colors all that goes on in the family. For his maximum sanctification, a wife must know how her role dovetails into her husband's.

Responsibility for the running of the home has been laid for so long on the mother that the virtues proper to her state are quite familiar. Recently emphasis has begun to be laid on the father's role in homemaking. Colleges are giving special courses in domestic science for men. Family welfare authorities encourage paternal diaper-changing, baby-feeding, pram-wheeling, and floorwalking. Some reactionary males are resisting the trend for turning fathers into substitute mothers, but the tide is strong. The ideal family man is represented as one who comes home from work punctually, helps mother at her household chores, works and plays with the children, and is generally useful and agreeable.

It is far from the purpose here to decry measures that bring a man closer to his children, especially during their formative years. The overthrow of senseless taboos regarding man's work in the home is a salutary movement. When there are many children a young mother without servants really needs her husband's help, so his participation in the household tasks may not be regarded as a gratuitous act of chivalry, but as his share of the home burdens.

However, we must not lose sight of the fact that man's essential task lies largely outside his home. And his redeeming virtue is (or should be) bound up with that task which represents (or should represent) his specific calling to serve God and his community in a very special way.

Divinely Imposed Penance

Just as a woman is hallowed by the divinely imposed penance of the pains of childbirth ("*in sorrow shalt thou bring forth children*") so a man is hallowed by the weariness and depletion resulting from hard work ("*with labor and toil shalt thou eat*"). Both of these penances have almost immediate natural compensation in the sense of accomplishment and peace they leave. Under ideal conditions the fulfillment and sanctification that a woman experiences through her family, while also accessible to the man, are secondary to the fulfillment and sanctification he can find in his work. The woman takes moral and emotional sustenance from her husband's love to spend herself on her children. The man takes moral and emotional sustenance from his family's love to spend himself on his work. Thus, in a measure, a man's whole family contributes toward the realization of his vocation. This work of his, identified with Christ's redeeming mission through regular attendance at Mass, is his most effective prayer. And while the family benefits socially and economically from his material gains, the atmosphere of the home is colored by the work he engages in, and everyone shares in the spiritual fruits of his labor.

Community of Vital Interests

There was a time when a man's family was very closely identified with his life's work. It was passed on as a sacred heritage from father to son. In Spanish there is a feminine equivalent for "baker," "hatter," "shoemaker," and it applies to the craftsman's wife, who was often his close assistant. In certain callings and trades this identification still exists. The woman who marries a king, for example, becomes a queen, with corresponding duties and privileges. The wife of a president, of an ambassador, of a doctor, of a small grocer, and of a farmer—all these women assume a certain dignity in accordance with the responsibilities which become theirs through their marriage; for in embracing the vocation of marriage they also adopt the interests and obligations of their husbands' careers. This adoption does not necessarily ensure a happy marriage, but it does make for a community of vital interests, which is one of its telling factors.

Man and wife need not share the same labors to maintain this mutual interest. There are certain vocations, such as that of the artist, writer, musician, at which a man must work alone, but which may take as large a toll on his wife's co-operation as if she participated in them actively. If he is working in the house, she must keep the children quiet and see to it that he is not disturbed. If he is away, she must busy herself with her innumerable duties, but be ready to drop them the moment he returns and needs to spread out his creation before the mirror of her eyes. If she is wise, she will impress upon the children that there is something momentous going on—something bigger than their own importunate and vociferous concerns.

Work That Shapes the Man

Other occupations may have less impact on the family's conscious participation and still be reflected in the home because of the man's genuine integration with them, or his wholehearted dedication to them. It is not a matter of higher or lower cultural level. It is a matter of work so designed for him that, while he controls it, it shapes him. It may even scar him, but through his voluntary acceptance of all that it imposes on him, it can ennoble him. I am reminded in this connection of Henry Morton Robinson's street-car conductor, in the book *The Cardinal,* who had a welt on his forehead from years of wearing a conductor's cap. In the eyes of his son that welt was a badge of honor, the stigmata of a cross long and gallantly borne.

There is no substitute for the feeling of security that permeates a home where the father goes about his work in a spirit of consecration. It gives an example for the other members of the family to follow in their own states, it sets the moral tone of the home, and it provides an incomparable growing bond between father and son.

Unfortunately today it is a rare thing. One of the paradoxes of our time is the co-existence of unprecedented freedom of choice of occupation with an almost universal absence of the sense of vocation. And the emphasis on monetary returns from employment is so strong that the work itself and its importance in man's regeneration are given minor consideration. Many wives are uninterested in the work their husbands do except insofar as it enables them to provide for them and their children.

The Charming Crook

Now if a man's work implements his vocation as a father, it follows that a man who practices an evil trade is a bad father. There is a sentimental conception circulating around about thieves and gangsters—criminals who "love their children" and are "good to their families." Champions of the lovable rogue and the charming crooked politician are sometimes naive enough to point to St. Dismas, the "good thief," as a possible example, forgetting that his goodness was born out of his contrition, which presupposes conversion. A man who engages in corrupt practices to obtain money for his family may act the part of the devoted husband and father; he may send all his children to Catholic schools; but "the sins of the father are visited on the children unto the fifth generation," and even if they should become saints it will be in spite of him not because of him.

These are examples of actual wrong-doing on the part of the father. Let us examine an area where the evils are merely those inherent in the system. What is the effect of the average factory or clerical job on a man's status as husband and father?

The Man with the Hoe

An interesting comparison was made recently between the undeniable slavery of feudalism and the more equivocal bondage of today's industrialism. The comparison was highly disparaging to today's worker. It showed Markham's *Man with the Hoe,* "stolid and stunned, a brother to the ox," going down to a well-watered grave, to be succeeded by the victim of a much darker tyranny. Drained of initiative and enterprise by mechanical monotony or benumbed by the boredom of irresponsible anonymity, the factory worker or office clerk seems to have fallen a peg lower than his predecessor. He has become brother to the piston-rod and the rubber stamp.

While this grim analogy has certain merits, it seems to me that it fails to give a clue to the real factor which enslaves the modern worker. It is not the drudgery, nor the quality of the drudgery, nor even the boredom, for all of these things may be involved to some extent as mortifications in work that can be truly ennobling. His thralldom lies principally in the fact that he is a wage-slave, a slave to the material compensation for his labor. Pressures all about him force him into this position. The unions, in bargaining for advantages for workers, have outlined certain terms: better pay, shorter hours, and other benefits, such as health insurance and paid vacations, *etc.*, which have become accepted as universal standards by which the value of a job is assessed. With every benefit having been squeezed from management by hard and shrewd bargaining, with jobs hard to get, with expenses mounting, and the perpetual threat of insecurity haunting him, a worker is in no position to weigh other considerations which otherwise should have valid claim in his deliberation. A few of these considerations might be mentioned in passing: whether he can take creative joy in the work; what his estimate is of the value to the community of the product or service offered; whether he will have an opportunity to participate in every phase of the production, or whether his task will be limited to a single operation; whether the work is sufficiently demanding to insure a measure of self-surrender, or whether it requires nerve-racking concentration; just how far economic necessity may be pushed as an extenuating circumstance for the petty lies, deceits, *etc.*, he may have to practice to get the job; whether the moral standards of the shop or office make his acceptance of the job an occasion of sin; whether he can have time off for observation of religious duties, *etc.*

Vicious Distractions

Since he may not ask these questions, he frequently gets stuck with the answers. Whatever happens, he has a job, the pay-check is coming in and he is supporting his family. To offset that "whatever happens," one man will resort to artificial stimuli; another to soporific escape measures. And the world which created these needs is ready to minister to them and furnish cheap and vicious distractions. Of course, we must not discount the mysterious alchemy of grace. A situation that will drive one man to drink will make a saint of another. But the situation in itself is demoralizing, and when industry becomes sufficiently aware of the inefficiency of an undermined humanity to institute widespread reforms, as it is now doing, we can be sure that the demoralization has gone pretty far.

Finally, it seems incontestable that there must be some relation between the level of ignominy to which fatherhood and paternal authority have sunk and the maimed manhood of so many workers.

A man whose work does not fulfill him can bring little home from it but his wages. He should be encouraged to do some productive work at home in which he can exercise his role of provider. It might be gardening, building an addition to the house, or some other occupation that will enrich the security and stability of home life. If the family's help is enlisted, it gives the children an opportunity to help father and have a share in his enterprises. Activities of this sort perform the double function of uniting the family and providing a vent for a man's creative faculties.

Fatherhood of Man

The cultivation of those domestic virtues which make a home pleasing to God is a great good, but we cannot stop there. It avails little for the members of a family to aspire to heaven within the confines of their home, if, when they step out into the world, their whole energies are directed to another end. For, in a sense, the whole world is a man's home, and all the people in it are members of his family. When he becomes a father, the character of fatherhood enters into his soul, and it should grow there until it permeates his whole being. It reaches maturity when he feels a sense of paternal responsibility for all the people with whom he comes in contact. He is blessed if he can exercise this benevolence chiefly in and through his daily work.

Any reforms effected by industry, since they are directed toward an increase in production and profit, are apt to become superannuated as circumstances change.

What is needed to charge a man's endeavors with fruitful vitality is a change of sights. As long as his goal is material prosperity only, any means used will deform him, for he was created for larger ends. Only when the goal becomes the carrying out of God's will can all his human resources be liberated and the meaning of vocation become clear.

It is asking too much of fallen humanity to expect that each and every man will attain to just that work (and no other) for which he thinks he is ideally suited. In one sense, the nature of man's power to adapt himself to circumstances, and his ability to triumph over emergencies, are too rich to be proscribed by the static limitations that such a state of affairs would signify. One of the elements of a true vocation is a humble acceptance of all the factors which determine it: not only personal choice, but opportunity, expedience, consideration for the rights of others (especially dependents), to mention but a few. (It might be one man's vocation to spend his whole life seeking out what God requires of him.)

The Helpmate

In the matter of vocation a man's wife can co-operate with him and help him acquire full stature. Too many women feel that they are helping their husbands only if they are instrumental in their material advancement. They maintain high living standards that compel a man to resort to sharp practices and cut-throat competition to keep them up. They use their personal charms and exploit the hospitality of their homes and the good will of their friends to maneuver for official favors, position, and power. They excuse themselves by saying they are doing this for the sake of their husbands or their children, when in reality they are joining forces with the slave-drivers who compel men to work at a breakneck pace to keep their heads above the waters of social and financial failure and despair.

If a man's fatherhood, to be fulfilled, must reach beyond the limits of his own flesh and blood, so also a woman's motherhood should overflow the physical bonds of her immediate family. She is by nature more solicitous for the demands of the children than he is. He is apt to be more concerned with the welfare of the community than she is, and sometimes his solicitude for the world at large and the part he must play in it may appear to her to threaten the security of her own brood. This can become an especially sore point if he wants to abandon the apparent security of a steady job to undertake some work which he feels is more valuable to the community or more commensurate with his talents, but which entails some risks.

The Problem of Security

One of the most important things for a wife to learn is that the problem of security is the man's problem. It is not for her to set up the living standards for the family, but to follow where he leads. She should not only cut her cloth in accordance with his means, but use all her ingenuity to give it the effect of abundance.

More and more young fathers are taking part in the do-

mestic affairs of the home. The woman should see to it that
it is a man's part which he takes and not that of mother's
helper and auxiliary. To accomplish this she must learn to
subordinate her will and her faculties for organization to his.
She is the natural intermediary between him and the children, but by deliberately effacing herself she can strengthen
the bonds that unite him to them. She has an endurance
that frequently surpasses his, but by leaning on his strength
she reinforces it and arouses his gallantry. (She may practice
extra efficiency when he isn't looking.) This is not coquetry,
but a voluntary mortification of her sense of self-importance
—an almost forgotten discipline that women must cultivate
anew if they are to restore the proper balance of power in the
home.

A Man's Work

This is only half the battle. For the rest, she must remember that her husband has a man's work to do in the
world. Whatever it is, her part is not to manage, or pull
strings, or criticize. Her part is a woman's part—to show
deep and genuine interest in all his activities, especially in
their human aspect. By all means, she should entertain his
boss and his colleagues, not in order to curry favor with them,
but to participate as much as possible in all that concerns
him.

Above all, she should do her best to enlarge his vision of
the work that needs doing in the world today, to encourage
him to do what he feels God wants him to do, and so help
him to become a saint and the father of saints.

OUR WORK CAN HELP US TO PRAY

Ed Willock

A man's proper view of his work has immense spiritual value. When work is well done, it becomes a partner to worship. The modern view of worship is to consider work indifferent to worship or even antagonistic to it. Work well done increases a man's capacity for prayer if he desires to be a prayerful man. Failure to work well decreases a man's capacity for prayer even when he wants to pray.

One element of Protestantism which survives the centuries and appears to grow stronger every day (especially, it would seem, among Catholics) is the fundamental conviction that Christianity cuts reality in two and sets one half against the other as eternal enemies. It is a kind of philosophy as juvenile as that of the little boy who divides mankind into the "good guys" and the "bad guys."

No doubt this view is a modern counterpart of the perennial Manichean heresy [from the sect begun by Manes (216-276), teaching that good and evil were two positive realities governing men's lives and matter was hateful—*Ed.*], an error so ancient and so honorable as to have been embraced for a time by the great Augustine himself. The reason

I tie it up with Protestantism is because the characteristic common to both errors is that they *divide*. Whatever unity is found in these cults is a unity set up against something else. Since the Reformation we have seen this fanatical warfare enter into every area of social life. The lone nation set itself against united Europe, reason was set against faith, the state was set against the Church, women were set against men. These are but a few of the innumerable contests instigated upon the false assumption that religion demands some kind of dogmatic partisanship.

In the midst of choosing sides some fairly fundamental values were overlooked. Dividing the peoples of the world into natives and foreigners (as nationalism does) makes us forget all about mankind, the universal brotherhood. Setting reason against faith (or vice versa) was done so at the price of religion which is a combination of the two. Marshalling political government against ecclesiastical government destroyed the social order which properly should incorporate both elements. The feminism which set women against men has destroyed marital harmony almost to the extinction of the family.

As long as this intellectual disease persists in epidemic form, every inventory of reality will be regarded as a list of contending forces. Every line of distinction will be a battle line. Each word of praise that is uttered will be taken as a derogatory remark against the *other side*.

This current way of thinking puts a great burden upon the minds and hearts of those who desire to go along with the Church in her work of incarnating spirit, reconciling differences, and uniting mankind. It is to this work of peace-making and unification that the Church is dedicated. When she makes her precise distinctions—for example between nature and grace, divinity and humanity, church and state, faith and reason—they are not drawn as preliminaries to a perpetual contest. Such distinctions are a prologue to partnership, collaboration, and functional unity.

If we are unaware of this unifying intention behind every Christian definition, then regardless of our agreement with orthodox distinctions our judgments will not be animated by Christ but by the divisive and competitive spirit of the world.

My concern in this article is to show how work, well done, has a proper partnership with worship, rather than being (as some would have it) a matter of indifference, or (as others would have it) an antagonistic alternative.

Martha and Mary

The gospel story which tells of the time the two sisters, Martha and Mary, enjoyed a visit from Our Savior is the story most frequently selected as evidence that work is an antagonist of worship. We are told that Mary "seated herself at the Lord's feet and listened to his words" while Martha "worried about much serving...came up and said, 'Tell her (Mary) therefore to help me.'" Our Lord indicated that Mary should remain as she was because she had "chosen the better part."

It is the easiest thing in the world to misinterpret this story and abstract from it that Martha was an activist and Mary a contemplative. This would be wholly unfair, since Christ's statement of preference referred to a single act not to a vocation. His sanction indicated no scorn for the hospitable services with which Martha was occupied. He did not advise her to cease her activities. He did not infer that one act was Christian and the other was not. He said nothing about there being alternative vocations. He did not say that the two ways of behaving were mutually exclusive.

Would it not be wise to read the story in this fashion? For Martha and Mary, Our Lord was at one and the same time God and neighbor. While Mary was answering the demands of the first commandment (Love God with thy whole mind...), Martha was answering the demands of the second (Love thy neighbor as thyself...). The lesson that follows from Our Lord's preference is that there are times when our preoccupations with serving our neighbor may blind us to opportunities (concomitantly present) for lifting our minds and hearts to God, the prior duty. It is left entirely to conjecture as to whether Martha continued to work and *listened* too, or if Mary continued to listen and *worked* too. Such a resolution, though not described, would seem to be wholly in keeping with the spirit of the story.

God and Neighbor

Is not the great difficulty of those who aspire to Christian living this very business of reconciling the demands of duty to neighbor with the demands of duty to God. Ordinarily the first commandment is answered by worship and the second is answered by work. The latter part of this statement needs to be clarified, especially in the light of modern living. It must not be assumed that neighborly charity is meant to be a rare emergency measure rushing in a pot of soup the day he moves into the neighborhood, or extending him succor the night his house burns down. No, the demand of neighborly charity is an endless daily debt that *can only be discharged through our daily work*. When seen in its proper perspective the daily earning of a living is at the same time, our daily exercise of charity to our neighbor. This point must be made strongly here, otherwise the largest segment of our lives will be given over to working for profits (if we are rich) and working for survival (if we are poor), leaving only holidays or the few hours before bedtime for the practicing of the two great commandments. In our day the attitude toward leisure-time avocations is different from that toward the daily stint. By associating the demands of religion exclusively with our leisure hours we rob religion of its vitality and we make it as objectively inconsequential as collecting stamps or practicing archery. To accept the capitalist wage-slave mentality that virtue only begins after the day's work is done is a guarantee that we shall forever remain ignorant of what is meant by either work or worship. Christianity is a way of life of which work and worship are complementary subdivisions. It is not just a method for investing one's surplus time and excess energies.

Before going on to show the relation between work and worship let's point out what has been said so far. First, that to set work against worship can only be done to the neglect of Christian living which is a combination of the two. Secondly, that to regard charity to neighbor (which is usually work) or love of God (which is usually worship) as avocations apart from daily work-day affairs, has the effect of making Christianity a hobby instead of a way of life.

Personal and Pressing

It can be shown that working well is a personal habit which can increase a man's capacity for worship. It is not easy to love God with our whole being. We must strive to increase our capacity for docility to divine persuasion. Two factors tend to weaken our efforts to be devout. First, that we find it hard to concentrate our attention upon a God Who seems to be very remote from us; we cannot see Him; His call to us is infrequent and faint amid the hubbub of life. Secondly, it is easy to postpone our response; amid so many pressing concerns we tend to put off worship as long as possible.

The second demand of religion is more intimate and pressing. Those who need our daily services state them emphatically and continuously. If we fail in our work, our neighbor is right there to point out our failure. The specifications for what we should do, how we should do it, and when it should be done are not left up to our lazy procrastinations, but our neighbor and his needs dog our every step. Striving to meet these obvious and everpresent demands compels us to grow in skill and diligence, and makes us *responsible*. We acquire the habit of responding promptly and effectively. If we fail to work and work effectively, we see the result in the deprivation of our neighbor. When we acquire skill and are docile to the demands of our work, we are encouraged to do more by seeing the obvious benefits which accrue to our neighbor. An example which strikes me is that of the housewife who exclaims, "I don't care to cook unless there is someone around to enjoy it."

Bear in mind that it is the same mind, will, and body we give to worship that we give to work. We are assured by faith that the demands of our needy neighbor are truly divine instructions as to what we must do. Consequently in responding habitually to these demands we are establishing patterns of behavior which are part of the divine prescription for our health and perfection. These virtues we take with us to our prayer. Good work habits increase our capacity for generosity, self-negation, and docility.

Concentration

As a father of a family of young children it is very apparent to me how close a connection there is between maturity and concentration. The child is a victim to his endless curiosity which draws him eagerly to one thing only to make

him disregard this interest for another novelty. In a matter
of minutes, the child's exploratory hunger leaves him no time
to lose himself intensely in any one thing. A selfish attitude
for drinking in experiences, tasting all of life's flavors, stands
in the way of the child's giving himself concentratedly to
work or prayer. He is the eternal consumer, the perennial
activist.

Among adults, it seems to me, this prolonged curiosity
for novelty and boredom with the familiar induces a
distractedness which makes it impossible for them either to
work well or pray well. Any skilled work demands concentration and singleness of purpose. This concentration is above
all a discipline of the imagination, so that only those phan-
tasms (pictures) enter the consciousness which are relevant
to the work. Day-dreaming is a kind of spiritual avarice,
amassing imaginative experiences as greedily as others amass
money. For a worker to decide to rid his imagination of every picture but that which concerns his work is a great act of
self-denial which increases his capacity for concentration.
Thus the habit of clearing his imagination of unwanted im-
ages stands him in good stead at his prayers. The mind of the
good worker is not one given to wondering whether he is at
his work-bench or at Mass. His faculties learn to take those
paths to which they are assigned.

Progress in Perfection

Perhaps you have noticed that in all this I am presuming
that the person desires to pray. I do not wish to imply that
work makes a person want to pray or that it cannot be a
distraction from worship if the person desires to be distracted.
Anything can be a distraction from prayer, even reading the
Bible, if the person doesn't want to pray. What I am attempting to prove is that work well done increases a man's capacity

for prayer if he desires to be a prayerful man. The converse is also true, the failure to work well decreases a man's capacity for prayer even when he wants to pray.

The director of souls will agree with the master crafts-man that one of the greatest obstacles to perfection is self-satisfaction. Of course, the director and the master crafts-man will mean something different by "perfection." I won-der, however, if they are not in agreement when they speak of self-satisfaction. Striving for perfection is an attitude and a way of acting which can be applied by the same person either to work or to worship. The man who strives for per-fection in his work is likely to strive for perfection in his prayer.

In the nature of things, working well implies a striving for perfection. For example, it would be a callous doctor indeed who could persist in elementary medicine if he saw more of his patients dying than becoming well; his failures would spur him on to greater effort in his art. The plumber who discovers that all his pipes leak would have to be inhu-man to avoid perfecting his methods of installation. Human misery is a great challenge to the worker, making him strive all the more to do his job better. That is why so many of us are opposed to factory methods of work that prevent the hand from improving his work but insist that every move should be precisely the same as the first. This induces a sloppy self-satisfaction in work effort, and one can expect that where such work practices are common the people will also be char-acterized by spiritual self-satisfaction.

Respect for the Medium

It is typical of people who cannot work well that they have no respect for the tools or materials they use. They try to drive a screw with a chisel, they paint over dirt, they try to run their cars without gas, they dust before they sweep, they try to force water to boil, *etc.* They have not learned to work along with the nature of things. Impatiently they impose their personalities, demanding compliance.

Work, which is meant to be the lot of all mankind, engenders a respect for the medium. No carpenter over a period of years would continue to slash wood, hacking at it like a demon, for no one would use what he made. The worker comes to realize that to get the most out of his material he must go along with the grain, so to speak. This virtue cannot be underestimated as an approach to worship as well as to work. The medium in worship is *human nature.* God wishes to woo our nature lovingly. Sometimes this demands firmness, at other times gentleness. The person who lacks this respect, however, tries to impose upon himself and others forcibly, unreasonably, ruthlessly.

At first glance this respect for the medium to which I refer may not appear to be important, yet it is apparent that the person who lacks this respect tends to regard religion as a form of "magic." Much like the impatient, unskilled worker, the person who looks upon religion as "magic" hopes to bring about satisfactory results with one vehement act of the will, one grand mysterious gesture. Thus you find people attending Mass in the hope of absorbing spirituality, presuming, it appears, that grace can revivify their souls without the slightest effort toward concentration on their part. This explains the common phenomenon of persons living in the presence of religion all their lives and yet never being affected by it. They have failed to respect the medium, their own natures. They make no effort at all to dispose themselves to grace.

They do not let work prepare them for worship.

GLORIFYING THE DAILY GRIND

Ed Willock

Christ wants us to be patient for His Second Coming: Science wants us to be patient for the triumph of human genius. Both promise true happiness, but one is lying. The "daily grind" of a man's work can be offered to either, but not both. The fascination of faith must not give way to the fascination of technological progress or else creativity, justice, charity, mortification, and Catholic Action will die.

Making a living is generally regarded as a grim but unavoidable necessity. The millions of people stirred to wakefulness each workday by irritating alarm clocks are not prone to leap out of their beds with a glad cry. The delight of a new day and the high adventure of living are not topics upon which many minds linger in the stumbling half-light of early morn. It would be erroneous to conclude that the present high rate of low spirits before the morning coffee is typical of man under all circumstances, in every age. It would be equally inaccurate to assume that men under better circumstances would not awake to something nicer than a vale of tears. These facts do not disturb us. The disturbing fact is that the rebellion which understandably grips our members as we rise from our couches has now taken possession of our spirits at high noon. Even in the clear light of day, with circulation restored, few men are convinced that the work they do is worth doing. They would be rid of it if they could. They feel "they should have stayed in bed."

I respect the exceptions to this rule. These may prove that *ennui* is not inevitable, but they do not set the style. Daily work is regarded by most men today as a necessary means to the end. This attitude could not have gained so many adherents were it not that grossly subdivided jobs have made each man's task distasteful. So many tomorrows of an awful sameness turn the tired heart to other sources than work for some pleasure, some adventure and some sense of importance.

The mood of the Monday morning commuter as he hastens to his work is not that of a free man tackling a job. The atmosphere of blue Monday that hovers under the droplights and over the typewriters is one laden with silent resentment and quiet despair. The contrived gaiety of the weekend must be replaced by the contrived docility of the job. All those who endure the monotony of specialized effort devoid of exciting purpose will recognize the description. The work is there to be done. The end and purpose of the work—that is not your concern. No improvement can be made in the efficiently devised routine.

The job is to be filled. That's the way they put it, and how accurate they are! The job is to be filled; the worker remains empty. The immutable laws of profit and technology prescribe the means and the end. If you fit those demands, the job is yours. No longer need your conscience be your guide, but let it be replaced by standard operating procedure. The conscience is tuned to God, but the wheels of industry are moved by the power of money and human genius.

The Promise of Hope

It is true that most people try to make the best of it. They wait upon events that will set them free. Immediately in their dreams is the next paycheck, the next weekend, the next vacation, the new gadget, but over and beyond this is the vaguely hopeful beatitude of a brave new world ahead. Despite the threat of hot and cold running wars, man's rendezvous with destiny lies ahead. We are told so in erudite volumes and in the comic strips. Our hope is in the future. Never look back!

In his book *1984* George Orwell writes a profound commentary upon our times by using the device of carrying current social trends to their ultimate; 1950's monotonous work and fear of being fired become, in 1984, complete automatism and terror of political liquidation. The powers which govern at that future date have discovered that the best way to enslave men is to keep them in such ignorance that they cannot conceive of an alternative to their plight. This ignorance is inculcated in childhood training where the memory is taught to forget. Orwell permits his leading character to become obsessed with the idea; he is plagued by the question as to whether at some other time things had been different. His inquisitiveness eventually leads to his being arrested, tortured and destroyed.

The point that Orwell provides for us here is his dramatization of one principle of hope. Man must look back if he is to gain hope for the future; man must look back because he has been sent. One function of the Church is to provide man with a tradition so that he may remember why he has been sent.

In her doctrines and history, the Church provides a rearview mirror in which we can see plainly a supernatural power made manifest in the affairs of men. This supernatural influence is the thing most lacking in contemporary affairs. The daily grind is godless. Yet there was a time in history when the presence of Christ was the most poignant and significant characteristic of the workday.

As we cast our eyes, first upon the ages of faith, and then upon the current science, we can see that the underlying impetus of living, which at one time swelled up from an awareness of Christ's presence, has been replaced by an impetus almost as mysterious, just as jealous of our credibility, but based upon human genius separated from the supernatural. Both of these creeds cast upon the screen of our imagination a vision of the future. The Church asks us to bear with this time of trial, expectantly alert for the second coming of Christ, at which time our fondest dreams of happiness will be more than realized. Science (the rival creed, not to be confused with science as a mere body of knowledge or a course of training) also quiets our impatience, admitting present difficulties, but consoling us with the hope of a millennium when human genius will control all power, dominate the universe and thus create heavenly circumstances on earth.

Both creeds provide us with a taste of the beatitude that lies ahead. We are not wholly bereft of contemporary consolation. Christianity reminds us of the presence of Christ with us here and now. Science points to contemporary miracles giving us comforting gadgets to keep our hopes alive until the triumph of human genius is complete

Daily Work Glorified

The daily grind can be sublimated by either of these creeds. If indeed human genius can eventually provide the fondest desires of man with complete fulfillment, then let us bear with today's drudgery, rejoicing in each new triumph of science, bowing before the signs and wonders of factory and laboratory. If, on the other hand, we know that Christ is here among us, meriting for us an eventual paradise of ecstatic delight, then let us bear with the drudgery of the day, rejoicing in each new natural and supernatural evidence of His love, identifying our will with that of His Church, the vehicle which bears us onward to paradise.

There is one thing that we must realize, however. We can't have it both ways! The two creeds are mutually exclusive. If complete happiness can be achieved in Christ and in Him alone, then human genius by itself has nothing to do with human happiness. If complete happiness can be achieved by human genius alone, then Christ has nothing to do with human happiness. Christ says, "Without me, you can do nothing." Science says, "Without me, you can do nothing." One of these statements is a lie.

The reason we must choose between the two is this. To achieve their ends, both creeds demand our daily cooperation. We must give wholehearted cooperation to the program if we want to be in on the "payoff." Our own personal pleasure must be foregone, and we must dream only those dreams prescribed by the creed if we want to further the mission of God or the mission of science.

Two Creeds—One World

Although there are two creeds (the belief that man's happiness lies completely with God as opposed to the belief that man's happiness is entirely of his own making) there is but one world in which these creeds can be lived out. Both creeds are concerned with the same problem, the satisfaction of man's corporal and spiritual needs. Thus two men awakened by different alarm clocks can take the same bus to work and even ring in at the same time clock, and do the same job; and whereas one subscribes to the belief that Christ is the source of all happiness, the other may be motivated by the belief that human genius alone can save us.

It is right here at the workbench that the complications occur. We must be very clear about the natural and the supernatural matters involved in the daily grind before we can see how society can be rescued from the false creed of science, and become aware of the presence of Christ.

The Saint and the Machine

In this one world where two creeds vie to win our loyalty, there must be some evidence, some sign, to which each creed points to prove that it is deserving of our credence. Each creed has a sign, an evidence of the power it espouses, of the testament it proclaims, of the hope it evokes, of the vision it promises. The creed of Christ provides us with two signs, the first is the Christian community, the second is the saint. The Christian community is a sensible evidence of the presence of Christ in the human community; the saint is the sensible evidence of the presence of Christ in the human soul. The power of God is made evident by the way in which it animates the human community and the individual person. The creed of human genius also has tow signs, the first is the industrial state and the second is the machine. The industrial state is a sensible evidence of the presence of human genius in the affairs of men; the automatic machine is the incarnation of human genius. Just as the Christian community and the saint manifest and bear out the will of God, so too, do the mechanized state and the machine manifest and bear out the will of man. Christ says "go," and the saint goes. Man says "go," and the machine goes. When this "going," this evidence, becomes a social thing, we have a society of saints which is the Christian community (the Church), or a society of machines which is the industrial state.

The Christian knows that the only way we can achieve human happiness is to subordinate man to the will of God, but this subordination is a means to the end of augmenting merely human virtue with the power of God which we call grace. By our humility, we will be exalted. Those who profess the creed of human genius tell us that the only way we can achieve human happiness is to subordinate man to the machine, but this subordination is a means to the end of augmenting merely human power with mechanical power, (or to be more precise) the power of human genius.

Sanctification and Mechanization

In the light of this analysis, it is clear that the two endeavors which concern the competing camps are on one hand, the sanctification of man and society, and on the other hand the mechanization of man and society. It is also clear why we see posed as giant antagonists in the modern world, the Christian community and the industrial state (Soviet Russia). One stands for sanctification, the other for mechanization. It is here that our dichotomy must be seriously modified. The fact that human genius has developed an organized rebellion against the dominion of God and that it has thus far succeeded in converting men and nations to its mystical blasphemy, may mark it as a sizable antagonist to the Church, but let us not assume for a moment that they are of the same stature. Human genius without God is a mean thing indeed, and were it not for the support its rebellion has received from the Prince of Rebels, its effects thus far would be most inconspicuous. The marked difference between the creed of God and the creed of man is that where one will redeem human genius, the other will annihilate it. Human genius may discard Christ and annihilate God, but Christ has come

among us to heal and uplift human genius. The war, therefore, is not between saints and machines, but between Christ
and Satan, between the Redeemer and the Destroyer. Nevertheless, the instruments of seduction are on one hand the
power of God, and on the other hand the power of the machine. The worker at his bench complies with these two
creeds. If it is Christ in Whom he places his trust, then he is
concerned about his personal sanctification and the
Christianization of the society of which he is part. If it is
human genius he trusts, then let him be resigned to being
one automaton in a mechanical state. He must choose the
power to which he is to be subordinate, God or the machine.

Profit and Power

The *ennui* to which I referred in the first part of this
article is a condition more hopeful than most of us realize.
We are now in a transitional stage. Momentarily the wage
earners are uncertain. Christianity of a past generation still
has some small hold on their attention but not enough to
reanimate them. The golden age of capitalism has waned,
and its dreams as well. The wage earners are not yet wholly
committed to any creed or ideology. They move more or less
from one immediate goal to another, not overly concerned
about the remote future or the final end of their efforts.

The age of profit seeking, in subordinating men to mass
production, has disposed them almost unconsciously to accept the mechanized state, and yet certain residual Christian
ideals of the supernatural and of human dignity keep them
from complete capitulation. It is of tremendous importance
that we see the situation clearly if we hope to seize this last
opportunity. Capitulation to complete mechanization will
be for most men not an act of enthusiasm but one of despair.

They will give up the struggle to reunite human dignity with depersonalized jobs, cash in their birthright and leave everything in the hands of the state.

Those of us who hope to see a renewal of Christian fervor must forestall this despair, and there is only one way that it can be done, by restoring a sense of sacred mystery which will touch men at the depths of their souls. This Christian sense of mystery is the only antidote to the maniacal rationalism of the machine. The fascination of faith must replace the fascination of mechanical power. If we concede for one moment that human beatitude is necessarily bound up with technological progress, and that man must reconcile himself to mechanization, we will only confirm the wage earner in his despair.

In order to illustrate this point of the need for a restoration of mystery and a scorn for technological progress, I should like to contrast briefly a Christian philosophy of work with the kind of attitude that currently prevails in factories, shops and offices.

Creativity

In the light of Christian revelation we see ourselves participating in a divine program that moves inevitably to a triumphant climax. This planet plunges gloriously and purposefully through space. God the Creator remains in constant loving communication with each of us, permitting our hearts and hands to develop and unfold the splendid pattern of His will. The most insignificant gesture we make at our work has eternal repercussions. In the name of God and the love of neighbor, we are bound together in the harmony of centuries and eternity.

God's love for us, and ours for Him, binds together God and humanity. This unity is creative, continuously generating new works of praise. The daily grind, with all its many acts and gestures, depends for its glory on the last simple judgment, "I was hungry and you fed me, I was thirsty and you gave me to drink...." Nothing is vain or futile or superfluous if it takes place within the orbit of creative love.

This is the conception of creativity that the Christian worker takes with him to the job. At his work, however, in many cases, despite his good intentions and consequent merit, he finds the workday organized along "creative" lines quite contrary to the will of God. His good acts and intentions are so many tiny boats struggling against the torrent which sweeps men onward to the millennium of human genius.

For the worldly credulous, "creativity" is the act of the machine. One mind makes the mold and pattern, then men and machines begin to churn and sway in rhythmic gestures grinding out endless duplications. Tabulating machines are the recording angels which transform many gestures into numerical "totals." The examination of conscience is an inventory of accomplishments—how many bricks, how many cans, how many sales, how many dollars.

The sterile "creativity" of the machine demands the complete subordination of the man. There are those who desperately defend this marriage of men and machines as a "creative" union. It is indeed creative, but in no sublime sense of the word. They say that a man and his turret-lathe are no different from an artist and his brush. This is as much as saying that a hurdy-gurdy man is as much a musician as a violinist. It is the machine that sets the rhythm, the pace and the contract. The man is a mere auxiliary control.

Do we rejoice in the works of man and God? A few people do, in the museums and the churches. The plaudits of the multitude are only for the work of the machine—the new car, the new television set, the new toy, carefully waxed so that no print of man will be on it.

The creative bond of love is severed between man and man, so that a new mechanized unity can be established. The automat (restaurant) is an ultimate. One man places a candy bar in a hole in the wall; another man inserts a coin which unlocks the door, and he abstracts the candy bar from the womb of the machine. Let's not kid ourselves, we like it that way! How much neater and more efficient it is to deal with machines than with men. The various brothers within the human family are ashamed to deal with each other, knowing that mutual creativity has been sacrificed in order to enjoy the fruits of the machine. It may be indelicate, but not inaccurate, to see in the machine-made contraceptive device a modern symbol for all barriers which prevent the seed of love from being fertilized. The industrial paradise has its own creativity which is not the creativity of love.

Justice

For the Christian the daily grind is a work of justice. It is the simplest form of filial obedience to the laws of God. His day's work is the ordinary way in which he holds title to his birthright. He serves God and his neighbor, contributes his share to the common good and provides for the needs of himself and his dependents. This is no mean accomplishment, because harmony and concord between all the various parts and strata of reality, the cycles of nature, human generation, and even the Mystical Body of Christ, depend upon a daily effort. Through his vocation the worker furthers the good of all creatures. He brings raw material to perfection by rendering it serviceable. He provides goods which are needed to make human virtue more likely. He obeys the divine commandment of service.

All of those magnificent gestures throughout history

struck in the cause of justice and freedom, depended ultimately for their lasting worth, upon the fact that each day
each man assumed his burden, worked honestly, administered wisely and cared for the weak. Social justice can only
begin at the work-front where wealth comes into being. The
existence of a social order requires as its basic skeleton, the
honest toil of workers.

In place of justice the industrial state gives us the work
schedule. Each man must do his share, but not according to
the rhythm of human talent and human need, but in accordance with the tick of the clock and the rate of production.
While thousands of families suffer without homes, thousands of workers sweat over piecework, turning out potato
chips, lipsticks, junk jewelry, paper napkins, neckties and
bombs. While thousands of unemployed sit morosely in
employment offices, new machines are being installed to take
their place. The rate of pay is determined by how many pieces
produced, not by how many children there are to be fed.
Every man must do his share; machines make tiny perfora-
tions in his card to measure his contribution. No question of
God, neighbors, or the common good—just production!
Rush orders to be filled! "Give it everything you've got!"
"Four thousand cartons of cleansing tissue to be shipped
before 5:00 o'clock!" "Everyone on his toes! Mr. Gulch wants
us to have everything ready for inventory before lunch!" "Get
this freight car unloaded—it's got to be out of here by three!"

Justice! What is justice, the in-basket, the customers, the
boss's wife, the production schedule, the timetable? Must we
rush because thousands are starving? No. Because thousands
are thirsty? No. We are rushing because the work schedule
demands it, and if you don't like it, brother, you know where
you can pick up your pay!

Charity

Work is an act of love according to Christian concepts. It is a better thing to give than to receive. At our daily work we learn how to be generous. We learn how to give. Of what value would be the monies of the rich or the coin in the collection box in alleviating the wants of the needy unless there were some worker, skilled through daily practice, to render the service that's needed? How could we feed the hungry without farms, millers, truckers, cooks, bakers, cattle men, shepherds, *etc.*? How could we give drink to the thirsty without well-diggers, vintners, brewers, dairymen, *etc.*? How could we clothe the naked without cotton pickers, loom operators, weavers, tailors? How, in fact, could we instruct the ignorant without writers, philosophers, translators, printers, book binders, *etc.*!

Certainly it is not to the isolated act that Christ will refer when He says, "I was hungry and you fed Me." We acquire the ability at work which, when accompanied by a response to the Holy Spirit, becomes Christian responsibility. Love is expressed in gifts. The worker is a giver, because he knows how to give.

In the industrial state where baked beans are counted and machines slice the meat, charity is replaced by service. Just as the Christian looks upon every stranger as Christ, the industrial mentality looks upon every stranger as a potential customer. The customer is always right. Why? Because he carries the coin of the tribute. (As time goes on, concern will be less for the customer and more for the government man. This has already happened in England. Ration tickets become more precious than money as rugged individualism is replaced by rugged collectivism.) But until that time, the customer sets the pace. Never mind feeding the hungry—they're all broke! Feed the gluttonous, give drink to the intemperate, clothe the debutante, house the gasoline station, harbor the wealthy tourist, instruct the G.I. with the loan, visit those who are in prison (they need lawyers), visit the sick and sell them insurance, and psychiatrists counsel the doubtful—it's a gold mine!

Christianity endowed the beggar with a certain awe because, simply and dramatically, what we did to him we did to Christ. It is this place that has been taken by the customer, and which will tomorrow be taken by the government man. These three have the power to move us, one by love, the second by money and the third by fear.

Asceticism

The most estimable quality of daily work is the opportunity it affords us to carry our cross with Christ each day. Good work will always have pain, callouses, sweat, failure and disappointment connected with it. In Christian terms these things are not merely negative. It is understood that an expurgation of our flesh is necessary before we can be docile to the persuasion of spirit. Our wayward passions must be broken to the harness of mind and will. As we carry the cross of daily demands we move toward Calvary and beyond that to the triumph of the resurrection.

Some Catholic sociologists who have despaired of finding any other admirable quality with which to bless the dehumanized factory grind, have seized upon asceticism as the significant feature. Certainly the monotony of repetitious effort is painful and difficult. "Can't we Christianize that," they ask, "and offer it up as an act of resignation?"

This suggestion that the worker accept the ascetic demands of industrialism shows a greater knowledge of asceticism than of industrialism. Those who have been more observant have noticed that industrial slavery differs from other historical forms in that it is an enslavement not of the body but of the soul. Only a man in control of his body, that is prayerfully and consciously transcending the ordeal, can volunteer his flesh to asceticism. Trappist monks, for example, through the habit of prayer, can silently stand to see their bodies chastised by fasts, silence, control of the eyes and labor. It is precisely this control, this invulnerability of spirit, which the industrial worker is denied.

There is nothing around the shop, no litanies, no abbot, no chanting of the Office, to sublimate the grind. Instead of swelling chants or the silence of the fields, the industrial worker operates against a background of urgent demanding sounds which threaten to engulf him if once he slackens his pace. The senses must be alert, but the mind is not permitted to make sense of anything. The one action that is impossible is thought. An animal awareness is there, but no cognition nor any quickening of intuitive perceptions.

This kind of asceticism does not free the spirit but destroys it. And please realize that the best industrial worker is he in whom the spirit has been destroyed! Let me repeat the diagnosis, because this is the key to the plight of the automaton—to sense, but not to make sense.

If the point is repeated often enough, some day it will be accepted; it is the end of the work which gives it its character. The end of industrial work has nothing to do with human perfection. The tone and atmosphere of the factory is established by its end. Today the end is private profit. Tomorrow the end will be collective power. The work will never be just, creative, charitable or ascetic (regardless of good intentions or holy motives of the men who may be employed) until the end of the work is the glory of God and the achievement of the common good.

Work Is Apostolic

With this point I will conclude, because it is in relation to apostolicity that the glorification of the daily grind is decided. Catholic Action will not have reached maturity until it has organically incorporated within its scope the motives and the works of people at the daily grind. Initially, the concern of the apostolate is focused upon literature, study clubs, indoctrination and lectures. This is natural, in that theory and spiritual formation of at least an elementary sort, must precede action. More and more, thanks to the Holy Spirit and the counsels of the popes, Catholic Action is touching the home, the office and the shop. This will save it from the curse of academics and the threat of angelism.

Catholic Action concerns itself with the problems of humans, that is, with spiritual and carnal needs. To the degree that the apostolate implies organization and the establishment or reform of institutions, it counts heavily upon the services of men who provide material needs. As I pointed out before, the corporal and spiritual works of mercy require and presuppose the vocation of manual workers. If the spirit and function of these works is to be revived, as the character of a revitalized society, then workers must be made aware that what they do at their work furthers or retards the apostolate.

Daily work for Christians should no longer be measured within the narrow limits of "earning a living" or "doing an honest day's work." The apostolic character of the work should become the norm. That is the point which I have tried to stress throughout this article, that work is at present organized to a specific end—profit and power. These ends have their own zealous apostles in the disciples of capitalism and communism. Christian virtue within this framework is sporadic and isolated, and will remain so until the workers know that Christians also have a theory of organized effort directed to the end of restoring all things to Christ in anticipation of His second coming.

If the worker is made aware that his daily effort can become great by its incorporation into the mission of Christ, we will have saved him from despair and rescued him from the destroying mystique of mechanization. To let him presume that his isolated acts of virtue (which are, be it noted, meritorious to salvation) will automatically reform an environment already organized toward a goal antithetical to the end of Christianity, is to betray him!

Practical difficulties have to be met, as I well know as a former factory worker, a head of a household and a partner in publishing a magazine. But practical difficulties are not the obstacles to spirited action but the stepping stones upon which we climb. Within the mystique of the machine the "practical" consideration is primary and that is why so many of us are more concerned about the practicality of progress than the mystery of redemption. We despair of our own powers being adequate to accomplish so gigantic a task as that of reforming the social order. Is not this despair due to the error of thinking that human genius can save us from human genius? Are we not embracing the enemy's creed when we dismiss an apostolic program as "impractical"?

Let's apply our Christian philosophy of work. Then let us organize with others to control the circumstances of our work so that our honest efforts are not perverted to profit and power. Let's immerse ourselves in the mystery of Christ's presence so that He, our brother worker, will help us drive the nails and lay the planks of a new order.

MONEY, MONEY, MONEY!

Ed Willock

Money is a necessity with which men must be preoccupied in the post-industrial age. The temptations of the money economy must be faced. We live in a society ruled by merchants. Because of this, no married man can be a St. Francis of Assisi today. Men must cultivate the virtues which curb money hunger: liberality, thrift, and proper reliance on God's providence.

Money is an enchanted thing. None of us cares what it is really. We are far more interested in the genie than the container from whence it emerges. Having ten dollars, for example, differs utterly from having ten dollars' worth of potatoes. To tell a man that "after all, money is just a medium of exchange" is as likely to change his opinion of the stuff as if we were to tell a child that candy is merely carbohydrate. It is not our thing (we moderns) to regard money objectively and dispassionately. Most of us are far too familiar with the hollow feeling of inadequacy that floods our being when we are broke. We are far too reminiscent about the sense of adequacy and power that comes of knowing that we are in the chips.

These psychological reactions to the possession or lack of money are far more relevant to morality and human happiness than the mere physical facts involved. A millionaire may (I have been told) feel utterly naked until he has at least another million to insure the first. Then, on the other hand, I have known poor men who suffered no feelings of insecurity unless they were without a few coins to jingle in their pockets.

If a man is money-mad or if he is completely scornful of money (both of which are peculiar aberrations left and right of center) his is a psychological and (possibly) moral condition not necessarily related to the amount of money the man has or is without. This is a vital fact to bear in mind, and an important distinction to make. Curing the physical conditions of riches or deprivation (both of which are to be deplored because of their harmful effects upon the soul) is different from curing money madness or money irresponsibility. The latter and not the former are the problems about which this article is concerned.

Enchanted Lucre

Money has produced cults (as do all enchanted things). The popular cult we all know. This is the body of the "faithful" who look upon being "in the chips" much as a militant Catholic looks upon the condition known as "being in the state of grace," namely, a condition of present power and profit and promised beatitude for the future. The purpose of the lives of these cultists points unerringly toward financial security with the same magnetic certainty with which a compass needle points north. Characteristically, a member of the catholic body builds his life about purchases which are strung out behind him like so many beads on a rosary. These people dread "being without" (it might be without almost anything!) just like a true Christian dreads sin. They know the price of everything and the value of nothing. They are most accurately described as "consumers."

A cult, with a much smaller membership, looks upon money as an evil thing. They flee it as something satanic, and in so doing comfortably escape the painful responsibilities that accompany its possession. These people are shocked that the Church has need of money (in the apparent assumption that the Church should subsist miraculously).

Historic Facts

We moderns live in a money economy. This is a short way of saying we customarily buy and sell things rather than exchange things as our forebears did. The present system has many shortcomings, but so far no better one has been devised. In a sense, a money economy makes for a society ruled by merchants. As long ago as the thirteenth century, St. Thomas Aquinas predicted dire consequences if such a situation arose: "If the citizens devote their lives to matters of trade, the way will be open to many vices. For since the object of trading leads especially to making money, greed is awakened in the hearts of the citizens through the pursuit of trade. The result is that everything will be offered for sale; confidence will be destroyed and the way open to all kinds of trickery; each one will work for his own profit, despising the public good; the cultivation of virtue will fail, since honor, virtue's reward, will be bestowed upon anybody."

Common gossip today confirms the predictions of St. Thomas. Personally, however, I am amazed at how many fundamental values have managed to survive in spite of our having to live in so tempting an age. In spite of our preoccupation with money, Americans are the most generous people known to history! An institution that has grown (and continues to grow) in America as it does nowhere else, is that of free, lay, organized services that subsist completely on donated money. I mention this to prove that here we have evidence of God's grace and man's moral adaptability. The situation is not uncomplicated. Vice and virtue thrive side by side. Living in a money economy as we do is not only a threat to Christian values, it is also a challenge to our moral ingenuity.

We Need Money

The temptations of a money economy must be faced. There is no escape for most of us. Detachment from money on the heroic scale exemplified by many saints of a pre-industrial time, is generally impossible to practice today if we accept a responsible burden in society. The counsel of poverty, to be properly followed, normally should be accompanied by celibacy and obedience to a religious superior. If we are married with children to support, trying to practice poverty in the classical sense will drive us mad. How can we, at one and the same time, desperately need money and not care for it? There is a way to develop virtue but it is not by that path, generally speaking.

By the same token, we must be careful in our application of ideas on money which pre-date a money economy. For example, the head of an institution (religious or otherwise) would be far wiser, in my opinion, to follow the example of Mother Cabrini in administrative matters, than St. Francis of Assisi. St. Francis did not have to adapt to a money economy; how he would have done it, we do not know. Mother Cabrini did adapt and achieved sanctity in the process.

It is wholly unfair to contrast our concern for money with the detachment of Christians who lived in a barter economy. Bear in mind that every society has its own particular temptations. In the Middle Ages, for example, the temptation to bloody feud and private mayhem was great because men commonly carried lethal weapons on their persons and habitually settled quarrels by direct action. The same was true of our early West. If people in those times were told that someday millions of people would live in concord, that one could travel thousands of miles with little possibility of being set upon or having to defend one's life, they would feel "such people would be saints." No, we're not saints. Our temptations are toward other sins.

It is unfortunate that we Catholics, by paying greater heed to ancient saints than we do to our contemporary popes, find ourselves with only monastic and pre-industrial admonitions about money that seem irrelevant to modern affairs.

We should face up to two vital facts about money: *1)* It is a necessity with which one is more preoccupied (and excusably so) today than in the pre-industrial past, and *2)* we can only escape becoming inordinately fond of the stuff by cultivating those virtues that will curb our money hunger. I shall talk about three of these which are particularly helpful.

The first is *liberality*. In my parents' day, the custom was to be bountiful in hospitality. Today one frequently gets the impression, that a tally is being kept of the amount of food one eats (if one is fortunate enough to be served food). This niggardliness in giving has become a social habit that is making paunchy, well-dressed paupers of us all. God will always see to it that we have ample supply on hand if we intend to bestow it liberally.

Thrift, it is said, is a virtue, too. It is. But as a virtue, what is the purpose of thrift? The end of thrift is generosity. One saves and administrates wisely so that one may be generous. There are still some people left who, when they are cautioned about their liberality say, "Well, after all, what is

money for?" May their tribe increase! No one manages money
more wisely than the man who gives it liberally. He has
adapted to a money economy, and what is more, he is happy.

God's providence is seldom seen in the proper light. It is
usually associated in many minds with a vague mystical notion of "manna from heaven." The normal way in which
God displays His daily providence for men (which we be-
seech in the Lord's Prayer) is the generosity of men, one for
the other. God doesn't usually send a sandwich, he sends a
good neighbor. We are all agents of divine providence. If we
are all seeing to it, each within the limits of his abilities, that
wealth is being equitably distributed, that no one within our
ken is in need while we enjoy an abundance, that we are not
hoarding for some portentous day while our neighbor is in
present want, then we are truly making God's providence an
obvious historical fact instead of a mere doctrinal platitude.

We must also prepare ourselves for the humiliation of
being on the receiving end. The myth of economic independ-
ence is a legend in which we have been instructed since our
childhood. Normally every human being is dependent upon
charity for a considerable portion of his life—in our childhood certainly, in sickness and our waning years generally,
in economic crisis often. This is the hardest time of all to
accept graciously our neighbor's ministrations and see in them
God's merciful providence. It is fear that keeps us from being liberal with our money, it is pride that prevents us from
seeking or accepting liberality when we need it. Both attitudes frustrate God's providence and leave us with doubts as
to whether it exists.

It is common for people of religious conviction, who
regret the dominant role that money plays in today's world,
to react strongly in the opposite direction. There can be
a considerable amount of self-deceit in this apparently

righteous position. If we will have no truck with money, we must also forego such responsibilities as marriage, parenthood, ownership of property and the administration of productive enterprises. Money, for a person who has no pretensions to luxury and voluptuousness, is a great cross. It is ironic that some people can refuse to bear this cross in the name of righteousness. Sadder still is the fact that these people who are wary of the seductions of money would, by that very fact, most likely be careful and liberal administrators.

Money (whether we like the idea or not), in an age when money is a necessity for existence, is a means to our salvation. It should be treated as such.

THE STATE, OUR COMMON GOOD

James M. Egan, O.P.

Of all possible human associations, two are essential, for without them essential human activities would be impossible or very hard. These are the family and the state. The orderly relationship of different family members is a good that is common to its members. The family is a common good–a good that is dad's, mom's, and children's, without belonging exclusively to one or the other. Societies similarly organize themselves in the pursuit of a common aim–Heaven.

Our everyday speech often witnesses to the fact that we have ideas about the state that are not only confused but verge on the erroneous. When we say, for example, "The state does this, or the state does that," we are thinking of the state as something apart from ourselves. A similar attitude is expressed by those who, for example, fail to report that they have become ineligible for social security benefits on the grounds that, after all, the government can afford it. They fail to realize that they are cheating themselves in the long run.

From this, it is an easy step to look upon the state either as an enemy or as a patron. When such conceptions become widespread, we have the basis for the notion of a "police state" on the one hand, or on the other of a "welfare state."

Unfortunately, there exist good reasons for such an attitude of mind developing in a people. What are they actually referring to when they talk about the "state" in this way? To that small but very important and easily distinguishable part of the state that *governs*. Now in our times many governments have presented themselves to the generality of their people either as an enemy or as a patron, depending upon how they have used the power conferred upon them or usurped by them.

Yet the government is not the state, nor is its function to be a policeman or a patron, though on occasion it may rightly become either. It is extremely dangerous, especially in a democracy, to allow such false notions to get a hold upon the minds of the people. Nevertheless it is not easy to explain the right notions, for they are based on principles that have not been very popular recently. However, we must try as simply as possible to build up the right notion of a state. To the pagan Aristotle as well as to the Christian St. Thomas Aquinas, the state is the most perfect natural product of man's moral activity.*

Much of what we shall say is also applicable to the supernatural order, but to avoid complication and confusion, we shall confine ourselves to the natural order. For the truth of the natural order is not destroyed but elevated by the supernatural.

---

* While we do not wish to consider explicitly the contemplative end of man, we must note that in reality it cannot be excluded. The end of the state is the same as the end of man and the end of man is contemplation, for by contemplation he reaches the Divine Common Good. Since contemplation requires that man be rectified by the moral virtues and enjoy a certain degree of external tranquility, it will become clear later in what way the state assists man to attain his ultimate end.

What Is the Common Good?

The primary difficulty lies in the obscurity surrounding the notion of "a common good." The phrase is used glibly enough by writers and speakers, but its meaning is so vague that it can signify almost anything the reader or listener wishes it to mean. An excellent demagogic instrument, and therefore dangerous. Already the notion of the common good is being falsely used in an attempt to justify euthanasia, sterilization and more liberal divorce laws.

The reader will pardon the use of a very simple example that will serve to uncover the reality that alone should receive the name of "a common good."

Note first that we say "a common good." For there are many; yet each one has, more or less perfectly, an essence that justifies us calling it "a common good," rather than "a proper or private good."

But to get on to our example. You, the reader, live in a small village and, at the moment, have two desires: you want to learn how to whittle and how to play ping-pong. By good fortune, there is a man living in your village, the only one, in fact—who knows how to whittle and to play ping-pong. You ask him to teach you these two skills and he is pleased to comply.

After the lapse of a suitable period of time, we find you possessed of these two skills, which you have acquired from your instructor. There are now two of you in the village who know how to whittle and play ping-pong. Are these, then, common goods? Not at all. Your ability to whittle and playing ping-pong is a private good which, it is true, you have acquired with the help of your instructor; but, if he were to drop dead right after you had acquired them, no change would take place in your skills.

Nevertheless, a further examination of the situation shows

us an important fact. Whether your instructor lives or dies,
you can go on whittling as long as you have wood and a
knife; but you can't play ping-pong by yourself!

Here we come to the heart of our example. To exercise
your skill in ping-pong (which is, as we said, a private good)
you must have an opponent. You realize (without difficulty)
that your instructor also likes to play ping-pong. So (by what
would be, no doubt, a quite informal arrangement) the two
of you agree to play ping-pong together. Now, notice that
word "agreement." By this agreement, the two of you establish a mutual relationship; this is "a common good." This
mutual agreement to play together may not seem to have
much reality, yet without it (in the hypothesis that there are
only two of you in the village who can play) neither of you
can exercise his skill or enjoy a game of ping-pong. This
agreement is not something one-sided. It exists between the
two of you; it is the good of both of you; that is why it is a
common good. This is the essential note of every created*
common good; it is a good for all those who share in it, yet it
cannot even exist unless it is actually shared by at least two.
It is not, as you might think, everybody else's good but yours;
it is your good and theirs; that is why it is a common good.

The Family, a Common Good

The common good that is the association of two people
interested in playing ping-pong together is obviously not a
very important common good, nor necessarily a very stable
one. It is good because it affords two people the opportunity
to enjoy a game of ping-pong; but needless to say the enjoy-

---

* We say created, for God is also a common good, or rather, the Common Good.
Yet the general notion of common good (something shareable without division by
many) is realized differently in the infinitely perfect goodness of God and in the
various created common goods. The Divine Common Good is a selfsubsistent, infinite
Good that does not depend in any way on those who may share its perfection. Every
created common good depends existentially on the parts that go to make it up.

ment of a game of ping-pong is not a very important good
when compared with many of the other goods of life. This
association, therefore, is not at all necessary; it can be broken up quite easily. The same is true of a vast number of
other associations in human life; they are more or less good
in as much as they afford an opportunity for the exercise of
more or less necessary human actions.

However, not all human associations are of this character; two especially are essential, for without them essential
human activities would be impossible or extremely difficult.
They are the family and the state.

While the common good that is the family is not the
primary object of our consideration here, a few words about
it will help us to understand the common good that is the
state.

The family is a reality, not apart from its members, yet
distinct from them. The family is not merely the juxtaposi-
tion of father, mother, and children. The family is something more than the simple sum of its members, for they are
members of a family; that makes quite a difference. The family
is, therefore, a common good—a good that is father's,
mother's and children's, without belonging exclusively to one
or the other. It is a good that is constituted by the varied
relations of father, mother and children. This orderly relationship of the different members is a good that all can enjoy
without any partitioning.

Moreover, the family is a common good in itself; it is
not a common good only because it provides food, clothing,
shelter, education, guidance and so forth to its members. It
does all these things because it is a common good; it is not
constituted a common good because of them. Even families
that cannot provide all these are considered by their members (if they are virtuous) as good. The family remains a

great good even to those members of it who no longer need these particular goods from the family.

Let us imagine, as an example, a family, father, mother, five children. One boy is a problem, a constant source of disturbance in the family and a disgrace outside of it. As he grows older it becomes impossible to consider him a member of the family. He leaves home and is cut off from the family. He may become wealthy, have apparently all that he wants, but he is still deprived of that good which is his family. (In other times, when people had a greater sense of the common good, ostracism was a severe penalty.) In this same family a second boy has had to go abroad for several years because of his job. He, too, no longer depends on the family as he did when a child; yet to him the family is still a great good and though physically separated, he is still an intimate part of it.

What Is a "State"?

The common good that is a family is so necessary for the very existence of men that God Himself immediately established its existence, structure and functions. He did not so determine the form of the state. Rather He made man a "political animal," that is, He made it quite easy for him to realize the necessity of larger associations than the family for his happiness on this earth and left the rest to man himself. Yet we must remember that God is the author of political society too through the nature that He gave man, which needs the state for its perfection.

The state is one form of society, the highest and most perfect natural society; therefore it will be constituted in the same way that any society is constituted. A society is a union of many men for the pursuit of a common aim. Whenever a group of men wishes to attain some common end, which they realize is either unattainable or attainable with difficulty, by each one acting separately or even as a family, they naturally unite their efforts so that the end may be more surely attained.

The society is effectively established or brought into being by their *consent* to unite; the union that results from this consent is the *society*. The thing that determines the consent, distinguishes the society, preserves the union, is the end that each and all persistently will and work to accomplish. An "athletic association" is a group of men who find in it the opportunity to engage in athletics; a "literary society" is ordered to the discussion and appreciation of literature; and so on.

Political society, too, has a definite end; however, this is not just another end that places it on the same level as other societies, for, as we saw, the end of political society is a necessary end—the happiness of men on earth. Political society is the communication of men, not for this or that special activity, but for *human* living in its fullness.

We might sit back now, feeling that we have accomplished our aim—the determination of what a state is. However, we are actually at the most difficult point of our enquiry. It is easy enough to admit that men gather together in political society to obtain happiness; but what is this "happiness" precisely and what is the relation of the state as a political community to it?

If we place the happiness of man in the accumulation of earthly goods, then the state contributes to it by facilitating production, distribution and consumption. If we place happiness in the progress of the arts and sciences, the state provides opportunities for their development. Of course, since these and many other things are required for man's happiness, the state naturally assists in acquiring all of them. Yet these things do not constitute human happiness.

A Life of Virtue

A happy life can only be a *life of virtue*. A happy life that is easily available to the majority of men is a life according to *moral virtue*. It is in the association that we call the state that men find the greatest opportunities for the practice of the natural moral virtues that make for happiness here below.

In an eloquent chapter of his little book, *On Kingship*, St. Thomas Aquinas points out that the greatest evil of tyranny is the corruption that it causes to the virtue of the citizens. Tyranny must be suspicious of all excellence in those subject to it, and especially of the excellence of virtue. We have been learning the truth of this by the sad experience of Germany and Russia.

If tyranny destroys the virtue of its subjects and is, consequently, a source of great unhappiness to them, how does the true state contribute to their happiness, to their life of virtue? By honoring the virtuous and punishing the wicked? Certainly the state should and does do this. But that is not the ultimate contribution of the state.

The state itself is a source of happiness by its very goodness; its establishment, preservation and progress make great demands upon the virtuous activity of its citizens. The state is a source of happiness to its members, not because it supplies them or gives them the opportunities to supply themselves with a quantity of private goods such as wealth, art, science, and so forth, but because it is an object so good in itself that it is the aim of their virtuous activity. As a sign of the truth of this statement, we should recall that one of the noblest acts of human virtue is to die for one's country, which means to sacrifice all private goods, except the good of virtue.

The state, then, is a good; it is now easy to see that it is a common good, for it is a good that exists only in the multitude of its members. It is not the good of one or another of them, it is the good of all of them. Each depends on the others for the establishment and continuance of this good, each enjoys it with the others. The state as a common good is not simply the sum total of the private goods of its members (unfortunately this is a notion that dominates much political bargaining); it is distinct from, though not separate from, each and every one of them.

To a person who thinks that happiness consists in doing what he pleases, the state may well appear as a "policeman" or "enemy." To the person who thinks that happiness consists in wealth and financial security, the state may appear as a "patron" more or less generous. To both the "state" is something other than himself. It is only to the person who acknowledges virtue to be the real source of happiness that the state appears as it really is—a great good that calls upon the resources of his virtue for its conservation and perfection.

Such a conception of the state is especially necessary in a democracy, which depends more than any other type of state on the virtue of its citizens. They, more than others, should find no difficulty in realizing that the state is the work of each of them and of all of them, that the state is the good of each and of all of them; that "government is their business"; that the state is their "common good."

THE HEROISM OF THE BIG FAMILY*

Ed Willock

This father of eight defames the character of self-appointed birth control experts who tell us how many children parents should have. He shows why it is wise and Catholic to have all the children God wills. He explains that the sentiment against large families is because we are too selfish to accept joyfully the responsibilities they place on communities and parents. Big families are the vitality of Christendom and the security of a culture against the threat of suicide within and attack without.

The father of eight, in a sense, is no more eligible to talk about the science of population than a letter-carrier is eligible to discuss the art of letters. Yet one must admit that nothing could be more correct than to say that no one bears the burden of literacy as literally as a letter-carrier. Though the mail carrier might be the last to consult about the quality of language, it would not be unwise to solicit his views concerning the quantity. He might even confirm as profound a view on the matter as that of Thomas à Kempis, namely, that men are entirely too verbose. I dare say, a letter carrier would feel this quite intensely, especially in the evening, when he set his pack aside and rubbed his back with liniment.

* First published with the title, "The Expand-Parenthood Association."

Following the same line of reasoning, the father of a number of children should have some views on population as a quantitative concern, if one is permitted to be so loose with scientific terms as to say that population is people, and, at times, children. It is on these terms, then, as a father of (statistically speaking) eight, that I enter the discussion of population. So that the side of the debate I have chosen will be clear, let me assure you that I take the affirmative, that is, I am in favor of people, more people, and preferably people who are unselectively bred. My method of exposition will be first, to defame the character of self-appointed birth supervisors who have the insufferable gall to tell parents how many children they should raise; second, to show that it is wise, as well as Christian, for people in a similar position to myself to have a goodly supply of offspring; and third, to show that bearing large families places certain responsibilities on the community as well as the parents; responsibilities which at present we refuse to accept.

Striking Example

I have a good friend who is a good father (and a better man than I). At one time, as most of us do, he had trouble amassing the economic wherewithal to keep his family in food and clothing. He had three children and was expecting another. One evening he arrived home from work to find that his wife was entertaining a visiting nurse in their sparsely-furnished living room. The nurse had come to see his wife as a service furnished by the local natal clinic. She was a smiling, efficient person and (according to the current custom) she had concluded that the wife was stupid, a mistake easily come by since the wife was extraordinarily courteous (a distinction far too subtle for the clinically-trained mind to cope with).

As he entered earshot, he overheard the nurse clicking her tongue over the rashness of further pregnancies, considering the precarious state of their finances. With that gift for direct action which less honest people can only envy, he solved this desecration of his home by a simple stroke of genius. He saw instantly that a meeting of minds was impossible and that some other approach was specified. He folded the evening paper quickly and then, approaching the nurse who had risen at his entry, he delivered the stroke (previously referred to) upon the ample but unsuspecting posterior of his unwelcome guest, while at the same time saying, "Get out! We have babies because we want them! Go peddle your drivel to those who don't!"

It is in the realization that mere argument is a far less fitting answer to the contraceptive cant of these home breakers than this direct defense, once so characteristic of Christian men, that I present my case. It is in the hope that fathers of families will soon take direct action and recover the right and regain the ability to govern their own homes that this article is written.

How Scientific Can You Get?

I have a good deal of respect for serious scientific study of population factors. I have no respect at all for actions either of a legal or educational nature which bring pressure to bear upon specific families to limit conception when such action is backed up by generalizations so tenuous as those presently held by population experts. Few sciences are so utterly lacking in evidence as those of human heredity and population. Apart from furnishing material for the Sunday supplement, it has yet to be proved that either science is of any practical worth. We would have heard far less of Malthus and improvisations on his hungry theme were it not that these doubtful sciences have provided aseptic white gowns in which certain childless and godless busybodies can masquerade as planners of a better world.

The ban on babies has grown so widespread in the United States that it might well be called a national anthem. Through the cheapest form of pseudo-scientific chicanery, it is insinuated that this country is becoming overpopulated and that to have large families is to do the nation a disservice. Unless, through some stroke of good fortune, one's children happen to come in litters or, as sensationally, provide material for a best-seller, the parents of large families are eternal defendants before the court of public opinion. Landlords, bankers and even the girls who ring up your weekly purchases at the supermarket, lift an inquiring brow. The ultimate in voluptuousness is not to have eight mistresses, or eight cars, but eight babies. The former excesses fit into the framework of the American way. The latter preoccupation is strictly out of order.

Amazingly enough, this replenishing of the nation's citizens is frowned upon at a time when a top-heavy, over-fifty population is howling for pensions and government vacation money. Who in heaven's name are going to do the nation's work and provide the wealth for pensions when parents are no longer even duplicating themselves?

Another interesting point about population is that the areas of densest population in this country, in more cases than not, are identical with the areas of childlessness. In the New York City area, for example, which has 21,852 people per square mile as compared with a density of 50.7 for the entire nation, about 50% of the couples enjoy neurotic childlessness, and only five per cent have as many children as are necessary to replenish the breed.

Curiosity is also aroused at the avidity with which the

president, during the last official war, sent greetings to two, three or four children in one family, once it has been ascertained that these candidates for cannons were of suitable age. Thousands of children from large families went forth to defend the right of thousands to remain childless—not only to remain childless, but by their injudicious and selfish buying, to precipitate an inflation which only increased the economic distress of parents with dependents.

Common Sense

It has been the custom among Catholic apologists, when defending fecundity against planned sterility, to make use of the *de fide* argument of trust in God's providence. This wholly legitimate form of argument has often been regarded by skeptics as a retreat from reason, as though an argument from faith were the last ditch stand of those who defended a practice they knew to be (human speaking) foolish. I maintain that to have a large family is defensible not only from the point of view of faith, but also from common sense. I also insist that to appeal to common sense is as much a Christian prerogative and as much a Christian custom as to appeal to faith. I am acting wholly within hallowed traditions of Catholicism when I summarize here just a few of the common sense arguments in favor of more children.

For example, if it is true that Catholics in America are more fecund that the rest of the population, and that they come nearer to replenishing their number than Americans as a whole, then this can be taken as historical evidence that Catholics desire that their faith continue, whereas Americans in the mass are indifferent as to whether their culture survives or not. Since there is no antithesis between Catholicism and the constitutional ideals of our country, we have further evidence that good citizenship when animated by the Catholic spirit has greater survival-value than a citizenship bereft of religious vigor. When one considers that the large Catholic family in addition to the burdens suffered by any generous family in a contraceptive climate also contributes children to an economically dependent religious body, and helps pay for private schools, their willingness to produce offspring is an even greater testimony to their fidelity and citizenship.

From another perspective, we should make note of the fact that the government is willing to spend about $5,000 to convert a citizen into a fighting man. If this can be taken as a token of the national worth of a soldier, and if it is agreed that the good citizen is as valuable, if not more so, than the good soldier, then the family that produces good citizens is doing the nation a service that can be calculated vulgarly at something more than $5,000 per head. Yet, during the 16 to 18-year process of educating and supporting these youngsters, the task is popularly regarded as folly, the families are treated by landlords as undesirable, the wage scale remains the same as though the father had no unproductive dependents, prices for children's clothing remain in the luxury bracket, and the government does no more than grant tax deductions, apparently on the pragmatic principle that you can't get blood out of a stone. I think it can be safely concluded that from the point of view of the good of the nation, it is wholly reasonable to bear and raise good citizens in quantity, but that contraceptive customs fail to reward or even tolerate this effort....It is not the large family that is hyperbiological (as the calumny goes), but the truncated family that is really reducing the home to the level of a stud farm.

Let Them Live

It can be observed, if we care to see, that the child con-

sciousness which permeates the large family presses a matur-
ing discipline upon the parents which cannot be artificially
imitated. There comes a time in the life of parents when the
presence of a growing number of offspring demands that
they, the parents, put away the things of childhood and assume the stature of adults. All the vain attempts to accomplish this same result by psychiatric counsel, therapeutic
hobbies, and the reading of uplifting literature, is tremendously more expensive and less human than having children.
The national consequences of the ban on babies is an ever-
growing petulance in public debate, cry-baby lobbying, lol-
lypop legislation, adolescent distractedness, the squandering
of wealth on adult toys, the identification of national vitality
with sugar and spice and everything nice. The dream of pen-
sioners to end their labors by 50, and retire in sunsuits and
short pants to some toyland for the toothless, is a rejection
of parenthood and grand-parenthood, an utter disregard for
the next generation, and a preference for being breastfed
rather than earning a living. From the point of view of the
life of the nation, parenthood and growing responsibilities
are far more reasonably to be preferred than this. A nation
that has lost its capacity for sacrifice is doomed. The nation
that can shout "Let them live!" will live. That's no more than
common sense.

I hope that my irony will not be mistaken for bitterness.
I am far too convinced that generous parenthood has the
capacity to survive the custom of race-suicide than to be
seriously dismayed at current irresponsibility. The nice thing
about a doctrine of suicide is that it is but short-lived. Birth
control inadvertently helps the nation by limiting the birth
of the unfit (the law of averages guarantees that birth-controllers become fewer and fewer). I am more troubled by the
fact that so many parents who desire and are capable of hav-

ing more children are afraid or are persuaded from doing so by very real economic pressure. The rectifying of this social evil is much more interesting and challenging than shooting at Sanger. So let's proceed in that direction.

Common Cause

The fact that strikes me as being most significant is that children belong not merely to the family but to the community. Please don't confuse this with the totalitarian doctrine that children belong to the government. As historical evidence of this we have the almost universal European custom by which all relatives and friends, especially unmarried aunts, uncles and godparents, lent continuous aid to parents and immediately fill the breach when parents are overburdened or rendered inactive. In normal times a European couple with four children or more would inevitably be aided in the home by an unmarried woman or by a girl of premarital age. Doctrinally, St. Thomas tells us that the venereal act is for the common good. If so, then it follows that the children, fruit of the act, are a community responsibility. In the nature of things, children are raised for the good of the Church and the good of society. Why, then, should the entire sacrifice fall upon the parents as though raising children were a form of self-indulgence and not a common good?

I realize that when I make this point it evokes in many minds an unpleasant picture. The popular sentiments are that everyone has the right to live his own life and that it would be unjust to burden others with the problems of parents who, by their own choosing, have "too many" children. There is a sense in which this is true and a sense in which it is false. It is false to the degree that it denies the proposition that the care of children and replenishing of society is the first responsibility of a society The entire community owes a debt to the next generation since it is through this new generation that the culture will continue to live.

Who's Responsible?

The sense in which these popular sentiments are valid is this: no specific person can be pointed out as being responsible to help families in a specific way. For example, no one can say to a single girl, "It is your duty to help the mother of the Jones family." Nor can anyone say to an affluent landlord, "It is your duty to reduce rents in accordance with the size of the families who rent your apartments." Vocationally and financially the single girl and the affluent landlord might be unable to be as generous as the situation requires.

This presents us with a peculiar dilemma. How can a community responsibility exist and yet there be no particular person responsible for discharging it except a few overburdened parents? The answer to questions of social responsibility, of which this is one, constituted the burden of the papal pronouncements of Pius XI. He saw it as the key problem of modern times, and as Father Ferree, S.M., points out in his pamphlet on social justice, perhaps no other crusade was ever preached as often or as fervently in the history of the Church. The care of its children is to the common good of the community. No individual, all by himself, is capable or responsible for the common good. The common good can only be achieved as an *organized* effort. It is a *shared* responsibility. In other words, when a certain common good is not being properly attended to, people must organize so as to be able to handle a job together that could not be accomplished by spasmodic individual efforts. Consequently, positive steps in the direction of helping normal-sized families ask new sacrifices on the part of individuals who are able to help, but *require above all* new, local and parochial organiza-

tions formed for family service and animated by the spirit of
Catholic Action.

For Instance

Some such organized services as I have mentioned already exist in some localities. I shall list a few and then describe some that can be especially effective. Parish credit
unions as a form of saving and a means for making loans
available to member-families at very low interest have been
recommended by the Papacy, and wherever they have been
set up have done much to relieve the economic burdens of
families. Co-operative buying, when animated by a Christian spirit of love and sacrifice, has provided savings which
make family expansion far less burdensome. A group of families in the Bronx have recently instituted an exchange service
by which high-chairs, basinettes, cribs, baby-carriages, and
even rarely-worn maternity dresses can be exchanged.
Baby-sitting services provided free or at nominal cost by
young fry have permitted couples to renew their acquaintance in an evening away from the endless demands of the
youngsters. If the young people won't do it, parents themselves can take turns sitting for one another. Maternity guilds
which solicit very nominal subscriptions from a number of
interested people can provide hospital beds, natal-care, and,
more than that, a Christian climate for lying-in mothers so
that childbirth will not be the clinical horror it has become
in municipal hospitals. Willing nurses and doctors could
sometimes be talked into such a scheme if mutual benefits,
spiritual or otherwise, were outlined to them.

Young men can prepare for parenthood (as a group does
in Brooklyn) by organizing a home-repair service. They do
over a kitchen or living room, brightening the life of some
parent, while at the same time becoming acquainted with

the challenges of fatherhood. Some young people spend good money taking courses in crafts and homemaking at which they learn far less than could be gotten out of this kind of neighborly service. Even the first awkward attempts at this type of service are tremendously fruitful in graces, maturation in group action, and valuable human experience.

A Radical Move

The point cannot be too strongly put that these organizations are designed not merely to care for a temporary emergency, but they are the beginnings of an entire social reorganization by which the world will be restored to Christ. The kind of organized neighborliness which the Church is advocating, *when accomplished and effective,* will have a far more radical influence upon modern life than the Marxist revolution. We must expand our vision to encompass revolutionary changes of which the exchange of a high-chair between strangers is but a faint glimpse. Family organization, when inspired by the Catholic vision of social unity in Christ, can become so politically potent as actually to displace machine politics, and to revitalize society with love for the offspring, not of its factories but of its homes.

Two far-reaching changes which present developments can lead one to expect are the decentralization of overcrowded city families and the restoration of the dignity of the mother. It is not inconceivable that the fathers of families could organize to build communities of homes in areas where workshops and gardens could supplement their present incomes. Everyday more difficult jobs than this are being done and greater sacrifices being made for ends far less worthy of human effort. My family and a few other families are at present engaged in just such a struggle. The obstacles we have overcome are no greater or less than any such group might expect. In terms of children, 21 now live in the country who formerly lived in New York City. By next fall this number should be augmented by eight more. Is our situation secure? What insecurity could be greater than that of a normal sized, wage-earning family living in urban chicken coops? What has been our greatest handicap? Lack of support from many who regard our experiment as folly, and slowness in acquiring group competence. What has been our greatest blessing? Help from a few who love children, and that modicum of organization we have been able to achieve.

Motherhood

The restoration of the dignity of motherhood increases as the home becomes the primary concern of the community. The statement that a woman's place is in the home has often been regarded as a prison sentence meted out by dominating males. An historical fact seldom considered is that, with Protestantism and private interpretation, the father became king and pope in his own home, and it must be admitted that to be so incarcerated was a form of penal servitude. To restore the Christian home would by no means imply the reinstatement of the patriarch-tyrant such as was found under the Protestant regime, but rather to emphasize the complementary nature of the two parental rules.

Within the Christian home, the mother achieves a status and prestige unchallenged. Outside the home, for the most part, the woman must frantically struggle to gain or to hold a status which is transitory and precarious. This country of ours at present is in misery and travail, suffering the interminable eruptions of women wildly studying, buying, preening, dressing, organizing, corseting and psychiatric-ing, trying to recapture the status which motherhood bestows immutably. Where husbands and fathers neglect their homes and community responsibilities, the same fever disrupts the family and mothers try to hide their motherhood behind the pancake mask of the free (or, synonymously, loose) woman.

It is said of the Mother of God, "Where Mary is, there is Jesus also." We can reverently paraphrase this truism and say, "Where the woman is, there the home is also." The mother incarnates the home. She makes it present. This cannot be said of the father (as anyone might plainly see if he dropped into a house where the mother was hospitalized, and the father nervously filling in). The father directs and defends the home. He ties it together with the rest of society. The primary responsibility of safeguarding the dignity of the home belongs to fathers organized for the common good.

Father, Dear Father

This prompts a question which is too frequently ignored. Why are there not more men in Catholic Action, especially married men? Why is religion predominantly a matter for women and children? I believe a basic answer to these questions lies in the fact that few Catholic fathers realize that their proper role as Christian men is to organize in defense of the home. They are chided for neglecting religious duties which often are secondary to this primary responsibility. (As, for example, joining the Holy Name Society or going to daily Mass. Not, mind you, that they couldn't do these things, too.)

If family values seen in a Christian light were once again to animate the customs, habits and legislation of this country, the traditional vitality of Christendom would be restored, and our culture would be secure from the threat of suicide within and attack from without. We could shout to our people and to the overpopulated nations of the world, "Let them

live!" We could weave the economic and political pattern of
social justice which would effectively implement the expressed
wish of our Lord and Master, "Suffer the little children to
come unto Me."

BRINGING THE CHURCH INTO WORK*

Ed Willock

Catholic men are so affected by society's prevailing
attitudes toward work that they no longer are aware
of the Church's attitude toward it. Because of this,
most men are unaware of any connection between the
Church and what they go through every day of the
workweek. Men can come to think the Church is just
an umpire that stays away from playing the real game
and that only yells out "Thou shalt nots." In this
article the wrong notions of work are cited and the
direct relation between the message of Christ and a
man's daily work proven.

The two most powerful ideas of reform in modern times,
Marxist communism and Catholic Action, have one point
in common—a great concern for man as a worker. The condition of the working class, conditions attributable to the
manner in which the mass of people work, have been the
singular concern of both Christian and atheistic thinkers.
Yet in local and parochial areas in the United States we select
almost any other facet of living upon which to focus our
attention rather than cope with the problems directly associated with earning a living. Home life, indigence, entertain-

---

* First published with the title, "To Dig I Am Not Able."

ment, play, and the conduct of parochial affairs are all being subjected to a searching analysis, whereas the manner in which the wage earner spends most of his waking hours receives little, if any, apostolic attention. Need we search elsewhere to find the source of our ineffectuality as Catholics when we remain so remarkably out of touch with the main line of sociological investigation? Can we presume that a reform of leisure-time activities can succeed while the workday goes wholly unattended? Since when has Catholicism become a leisure-time activity?

Three Theories of Work

As Catholics, our reluctance to give ample consideration to men as workers has resulted in leaving the establishment of a philosophy of work up to the capitalist, the communist and the bohemian [*i.e.,* the theory of work believed by those of artistic and literary interests who disregard conventional standards of behavior–*Ed.*]. Each of these three schools of thought contributed largely to what have become the popularly accepted attitudes toward work. These attitudes can hardly be questioned, so entrenched have they become, yet on careful examination it is obvious that they take little, if any, direction from Christianity. Consequently the wage-earning Catholic, along with his non-Catholic fellow workers, must subscribe to a wholly secular conception of work or else have no higher ideals in the matter than that of a beast foraging for sustenance. That there is a Christian philosophy of work which is one of the great heritages of Western culture, and which at the same time served as foundation for European civilization, is an historical fact known to few. It is small wonder then that the working man sees a gulf between himself and the Church, if he is unaware that there is any relevancy between Catholicism and the daily grind. It

is unlikely that the influences to which he is hourly subjected every day of the week will be dispelled by Sunday
sermons, especially if he is unaware of the direct relation
between the message of Christ and his daily work. He can
hardly help but conclude that religion is a sort of umpire
that remains aloof from the game except to interject uncom-
fortable "Thou shalt nots" if he has not learned that Christianity is meant to be a wholly involved animating spirit
within human work.

I might well take my key from the Church in writing
this article, and begin my discussion of work by renouncing
these particular devils that have come to possess the secular
notion of work. I have attributed these false notions to three
sources: the capitalist, the communist, and the bohemian.
In speaking of these as three schools of thought, I endow
them with a greater formality than generally known to their
disciples. The average guy one meets has never perhaps identified the sources precisely, yet he has, almost through a process of osmosis, absorbed work notions attributable to these
three schemes of living. The average wage earner might actually renounce either of these three and yet inadvertently
be in their debt for his training. It is well to bear in mind
that it is humanly impossible to be as sterile of ideas as the
cartoonist's American is supposed to be. It is our habit as a
people to deny the source of our ideological being, yet obviously the notions we possess must have come from some-
where. They were not, as the Irish say, just licked off the
grass.

Capitalism's Attitude Toward Work

Industrial capitalism, as it reached maturity, was hard
put to invent a philosophy to justify its existence. Since it
knew no other source from which to borrow respectability,

it took some spiritual concepts from Christianity and twisted them to suit its purpose. The situation it felt called upon to justify, was the obvious mal-distribution of wealth, which compelled most men to work at unrelieved drudgery while a few wallowed in profitable inactivity. To soothe bothered consciences so as to make capitalistic comfort complete, it invented a notion of work which would console rich and poor alike. Thus came into being the notion which quieted the laboring classes, namely, that drudgery was designed by an all merciful God as a means by which sinners might painfully discharge the debt accrued by their sins. This notion conveniently passed religious inspection simply because it happened to be half true. The notion which followed from this as night follows the day, was that the man of prosperous inactivity was so because of his virtue. Wealth, in as much as it freed a man from servility, became a mark of election. It was in this way that work became identified with sin, and means became identified with virtue, a notion which endures, with less theological support, up unto the present day. Manicured finger nails and well-creased clothing continue to be a mark of election, and hard labor is looked upon as a penalty for crime. Unionists seem to seek insatiably for less work and more leisure. The wage earner endures the week's pain only in the hope of weekend beatitude. Vacation spots are called "paradises." We imagine saints as being fairly inactive people. In his spare time the laborer dons the garb which the well-to-do wear daily and flees to spots where he can be attended by flunkies.

The Other Side

The communist does not like to work either. He regards it as an injustice that bananas must be picked and peeled before they are eaten. Although he has a predilection for overalls, he likes them creased. He agrees with the capitalist that vacationland is a paradise; his sole gripe is that paradise has a cover charge. His basic revolt is against creatureliness. He balks at necessity and envies the god who can do things gratuitously, without compulsion or effort. The Soviet Park of Culture and Rest is another Central Park, an Arboretum of Atrophy. An elaborate disdain for honest sweat prompts him to seek the perfumed couch of affluence. His solution to the problem of men standing on top of one another is to put everyone on top and let men stand in midair, in imitation of medieval paintings of the Communion of Saints.

How the Bohemian Feels

The bohemian revolted against the economics of the capitalist and the politics of the communist. He also revolted against the constrictions of Christianity. He is, to put it simply, a revolting person. In order to justify his existence as a non-participant in gainful employment, he felt called upon to insist that work is mainly a form of self-expression in no way related to the crass necessity of filling one's stomach. He broke up the marriage between necessity and invention, implying that the only honorable motivation for human labor is an unsuppressible spiritual burp. At one time the bohemian called this motivation "inspiration." As an animating force it was not unlike certain "religish" people's reference to the Holy Spirit. Practically, in both cases, it serves as a cover-up for a stubborn determination to get their own way and do as they darn well please.

The bohemian's only criterion for measuring work is that it be satisfying—to him. He poses this self-satisfaction as being honorable as compared with the compulsion of corporal necessity. In his mind the artist is the only true worker.

The artist is moved by no definable compulsion, whether it be courtesy or justice. If he must work, then it is for the same reason that a sneezer must sneeze. That is why the visitor to salons of current art, after seeing the art objects, feels as though someone had sneezed in his face.

To Work Ourselves Out of it

Summarily, all these three opinions of work generally held in some mixture by the average man today, have this one point in common; we work only to be free of the necessity of working. Working is a way of relieving oneself either of corporal necessities or emotional compulsions. The state of non-working is regarded as more dignified and preferable to that of diligence.

It is unfortunate that any individual who accepts the bohemian, capitalistic or communist ideas of work will find in most of our towns and cities an active group of people more than ready to go along with him, whereas the convinced Christian worker will generally find himself to be alone and lonely in his views. Christian convictions in regard to work are socially unconfirmed. The sacrament of mature Christianity has not yet replaced infantile ethics in our religious scheme of things. As a result of this, much like the early Christians, individuals must seek confirmation of their views not in their local surroundings, but in literature sent out by wandering apostles. The writings of Eric Gill and Fr. McNabb, O.P., have gone far toward describing new directions in this field of work....

The Christian Scheme of Work

The Christian philosophy of work was developed over a period of more than fifteen centuries, whereas the philosophy behind modern work is hardly three centuries old. Consequently, to the modern mind, Christian notions of work are both strange and elaborate. Since it would be impossible to do justice in a few pages to a system that represents many centuries of development, I have chosen to discuss only a few Christian notions of work that differ most remarkably with those currently held.

We have been reminded by the popes that it is as natural for man to work as it is for birds to fly. In other words, creative activity is essential to human perfection. It is not merely the result of sin or his fallen nature. To identify work with the drudgery, disappointment, and frustration that usually accompany it is a gross error. Admittedly all this unpleasantness is a chastisement for sin, yet there is far more to work than just pain. The farmer not only sweats and strains, he also produces wheat and cabbages. The concert violinist may lose six pounds as he perspires through his concert, but his audience did not come just to watch his agony; they came to enjoy his music. Work normally involves a good deal of drudgery, but drudgery is not the essence of work. The birth of a child has its labor pains, but these pains are soon forgotten in the delight that another child has been born. The fault, for example, with much factory labor is not that there is drudgery connected with it, but that there is nothing but drudgery connected with it. Instead of being a daily nativity, it is usually just a daily abortion—all pain and no fruit.

It has been traditionally understood that man at his work is an instrument of God's providence. We have been created as agents of our own survival and perfection. The way in which God provides for mankind's needs is through mankind's labor. When we pray for our daily bread we do not expect a shower of ham sandwiches from heaven. This is not the usual method of providence. We do expect, when we pray for bread, to receive our share of the fruits of human labor. Man's daily work is the daily instrument of divine providence.

Creation as a Necessity

A point that should be clarified here is the relation between necessity and gratuity in creative activity. Gratuity may be an unfamiliar word, but by definition it means without compulsion or without necessity. Christianity teaches that our perfection must be built upon our being creatures. A creature is a thing of needs, just as a creator, strictly speaking, is one who needs nothing. As human beings, we need God, we need each other, we need food, clothing, shelter and many other things. Since God is all powerful, all knowing and all merciful, having need of Him is a strength, not a weakness. The man who resents necessity is, in fact, cursing his very existence. He who would be free of necessity, never compelled to pray, work, or love, desires to be God. He is a presumptuous fool.

This creaturely necessity is a thing we share also with the beasts. Does this imply that human effort is a beastly thing, not too different from the activity of ants or beavers? No! Human work, because it is a co-creative rational activity, possesses a kind of divine spark. True, a man just like a beast can be prompted to work simply by his stomach, but he can also be moved to effort in the same fashion that God is moved—through love. The Christian dispensation favors us with the privilege of working intimately and familiarly with God. Our work can now be done in the company of Christ, not prompted solely by beastly necessity, but by gratuitous love of our brothers in Christ! Thus you see, our Brother Christ perfects the law of human necessity by making it the occasion for supernatural charity. The Christian can rejoice in the compulsion to work because the compulsion to work is a call to love as God loves. God's creative acts are acts of love; also, thanks to Christ, our co-creative acts can be an extension of this same divine love!

Working Together

One of the unfortunate notions which we picked up during the nineteenth century, an inheritance from the Renaissance, is the conviction that only the work of the individual artist can be truly creative. This is utter nonsense! The most usual and normal kind of work is collaboration. Most men in all ages have worked together daily to produce some common good. The lone worker has always been the exception. It is true that the enormous subdivision of work devised by our factories, provoked by profit regardless of the good of the worker, has become so grotesque that it can hardly be regarded as work at all. It might be better defined as a penance. Yet a certain subdivision of work is not only normal, but often to be preferred. For example, who would prefer a one-man band to a symphony orchestra? Would it have been preferable that the Cathedral at Chartes be raised by one man? Which is the greater work of genius, a Shakespearean sonnet or the English language? Remember that symphonic music, cathedrals and languages, all human artifacts, were the products of men working together.

It is well to keep the above point in mind, especially when we are considering social reform. The reformers are doomed to disappointment who imagine that the restoration of creative work means to provide each worker with his own individual studio. Work can be done by teams of free men and it is such collaboration that could practically replace today's crews of wage-slaves.

Nice Work—If You Can Get It

Millions of workers today are involved in mechanical labor to which a Christian philosophy of work cannot be applied. Whatever the worker's will in the matter might be, the end and methods of the work have been already prescribed. Accept it he can, as a penance, but no amount of acceptance as a penance will convert it into co-creative work. Wage earners so involved are inclined to laugh at the Christian philosophy of work because it seems so far-fetched and impracticable—for them.

Personally I am more concerned about the mass of wage earners than I am about lone artists. I refuse to admit that the present state of affairs is unchangeable. Man devised the factory method, so man can replace it with something better. It will be far less difficult to change the work system than it will be to restore souls to Christ. As Catholics we are pledged to the latter, so perhaps we can make the former reform a by-product of our apostolic efforts.

To my mind there is only one great reason why persons otherwise convinced permit their workday to be vitiated by secular methods of work; they lack the will to do otherwise. I do not put the blame wholly upon the individual who finds himself swallowed up in the factory-office rat race; my reference is to a common will. To make myself clear about this common will, let me point out that there are many good things that cannot be accomplished by individuals alone, no matter how strong their intentions. No one person can, for example, decide to raise a family; at least two will are required to make such a decision. No one person can decide to build a community; it requires many wills, a common will, to accomplish so complicated a task. Christians today lack the common will to reform the workday. They are deterred from their good intentions by any enumeration of the difficulties involved.

I cite as evidence of this lack of common will the fact
that our schools, even Catholic schools, generally prepare us
for secular employment by failing to prepare us for Christian service. As children we are given neither the enthusiasm
nor competence to earn a living through honest and skillful
service. If the thousands who graduate from our Catholic
schools and colleges were all prepared and competent to render honest service, and were then frustrated from doing so
by an unsympathetic secularism, I would agree that the ideal
was impracticable. The fact is that thousands of Christian
wage earners must confess with the unjust steward, "To dig
I am not able," and it is this incompetence which forces
them to accept capitalist, communist, and bohemian standards of work.

FORWARD TO THE LAND*
Ed Willock

To imply that the spot in which a family currently finds itself is the providential spot in which it should remain is ridiculous. Contrary to city life or money-conscious suburbia, living in the country imposes a logic within which all other matters are better measured in their Catholic context. The author addresses the inevitable issues regarding a move forward to the land, *i.e.,* escapism, romanticism, children, property, neighborliness, and "abandonment" of apostolic responsibilities.

The subject of decentralization (or returning to the land) is one that holds interest for two classes of people: those who find the subject entertaining, and those who find the actual situation challenging. It can be safely presumed that nine out of ten who are articulate on the subject have no intention whatever of doing anything about it. It is vital to distinguish between the two types of discussion because material dear to the heart of one group will be looked upon as irrelevant by the other and, of course, vice versa.

Those who pursue the subject as a form of entertainment talk of rural living as though it were an end in itself. Those who are curious because they really intend to move

---

* First published with the title, "Flight From the City."

from the city, or at least have grave misgivings as to whether city living is for them, see decentralization as a means to an end. Thus, for example, whereas some imply that the presence of a compost heap on one's acre, or the smell of a barn, automatically evokes the best in human nature, other devotees of the subject will regard compost heaps as a means for producing cheap and excellent fertilizer and will place barn smells in a similar category with gasoline fumes as environmental nuisances to which the native quickly becomes accustomed.

It is not my intention to wag a scornful finger at those who merely find entertainment in the subject. I merely desire to warn the person who is actually interested in living in the country that much of what has been said about back-to-the-land movements is utterly irrelevant to the practical problem. Two such points of irrelevancy, for example, are (1) the assertion that there is something anachronistic, medieval or old-fashioned about preferring to live in the country rather than on the fringes of industrial installations, and (2) that a Catholic who leaves the city for the country is deserting his apostolic post or (to be European) fleeing his milieu.

Escapists?

The man who has never encountered these two assertions is fortunate, but I am told that such arguments hold weight with many Catholic people who have discussed the matter. The first assertion is just not true. The exodus from large cities has been going on for a long time in this country. As a social movement it is utterly contemporary. The population of many of our large cities is decreasing, and a tour through the American countryside reveals a feverish epidemic of house building. More and more people every day are taking to gardening and raising livestock, or engaging in home industries. The sad fact is, however, that this exodus is being made in the main by small families of more than average income, leaving behind in the cities the large families of low income who would benefit much more by such a change. Most of those Catholic couples who have large families are in this category of low-income, propertyless city dwellers. The problem, then, is to devise a social program by which the families who need them most can find homes and property in the country at prices commensurate with their incomes. Once there, with a little ingenuity, home gardens, livestock and home industries will supplement their incomes, making it possible to enjoy a more abundant life than could have been possible within the city.

The second assertion—that moving from the city is to desert one's apostolic post—is a glaring example of the common error of applying European norms to the American scene. The average American family changes its place of habitation at a great clip. Almost as frequently do our wage-earners change their jobs. It is rare to find a family, all of whose members remain native to a particular town, or who gain their livelihood from the same kind of occupation. Within the limits of our vast borders we are a highly nomadic people. Ours is an ever-changing milieu. Our personal and family life is a chain of episodes bound together by moving vans and employment agencies. However regrettable this may be, it is the fact of the matter. To imply that the spot in which a family currently finds itself is the providential spot in which it should remain, is as ridiculous as to assert that the person with whom you happen to be dancing at a masked ball at the stroke of midnight should be your partner for life.

No Desert Island

When a family moves from the city, the greatest likelihood is that intimacy with neighbors and participation in political, parochial and social affairs will increase. I hasten to add that no one in his right mind advocates that an individual or a family should flee the city and take up residence in an isolated retreat like a voluntary *Swiss Family Robinson*. The decentralized family will either move to the land in company with others, or else move into an already existent rural community. In such places it will soon be discovered that rural people do not tolerate the inbred individuals who "want to be alone." It is far more likely that in the country the individual will find himself in an environment in which he is comprehended and which is comprehensible to him. Perhaps for the first time in his life he will experience the joy of being a man among men, rather than being a lonely pebble on a vast beach. In the majority of cases an exodus from the city will not be a fleeing of one's milieu but rather a discovery of neighborliness.

I hold, then, that the arguments of anachronism or desertion of milieu are irrelevant to the practical consideration of moving to the country. To proceed to considerations which I believe are relevant, and usually ignored, I wish to discuss four.

The Romantic Aspect

The revolt against the sordidness of the industrial metropolis began about the same time that thousands of "yokels" took it into their heads to go to the big city and make good. Not infrequently the rural-bound "slicker" would encounter the city-bound "yokel" as they passed, going in opposite directions. Whatever romantic notions they held in regard to their points of destination were held up to the biting ridicule of the disillusioned. Thus it came to be that romantic arguments lost disfavor to be replaced by hard, eco-

nomic facts. No one dared say that he admired the countryside for its peace, its robustness or its beauty. No one dared
admit that he loved the city for its hustle, its bright lights, its
defiance of elemental nature. Yet I contend that these so-
called "romantic" features are the deciding factors in one's
preference. I am convinced that those who have succumbed
to the enchantment of bright lights and the society of the
herd will never be happy in the country, regardless of its
more tangible benefits. One the other hand, the person who
has fallen in love with the prospect of "man in a landscape"
and the sweet-sour taste of elemental nature will never be
happy in the city.

Chesterton spoke of his preference for sitting in a field
watching the cars go by, rather than sitting in a car watching
the fields go by. This kind of preference is what I'm talking
about. Anyone is likely to enjoy looking at natural beauty,
but the true countryman desires to be touched and affected
by nature. Some protection from the elements is desirable,
but he who wishes to carry this security to the point of complete insulation so that (in a manner of speaking) he sees
nature only through a window will be happy only in the city.

Few facts have been so splendidly defended by empirical
evidence as the economic, cultural, familial, social and health-
ful benefits of life in the fields, yet how few are they who
have been convinced? Why? Because (I think) the city enchantment refuses to be dispelled by such arguments. It must
be admitted that the variety of merchandise available in the
city shop is far more glamorous than the limited monoto
nous staples grown in one's own garden. It must be admitted
that there is a fascination in spending one's day among innumerable strangers which is not the same as seeing the same
familiar faces every day in the week. There is a sense of dominion in knocking on the apartment pipes for more heat

which is not found in cleaning out one's own ashes. He who can afford a city breakfast of bacon and eggs can wallow in a sense of accomplishment as he wields his knife and fork, a gratification which the countryman feels bound to share with the chicken and the pig, however humiliating it may be.

The country has its romance and the city has its enchantment, and the price of trying to have both produces the money-conscious dissatisfaction of the suburbs. In the nature of things these delights are alternatives. From the two moves, one is the deciding factor as to the place where one finds contentment. This is not to imply that one is cut out by nature to be inevitably a city-dweller or a rustic. My point is that—considering the life to which he has become conditioned—the process by which the city-bred is persuaded to go to the land is less a re-education than a disenchantment. The appetites he has acquired will not be gain-said by arguments of health, stability or economics. His false gods must be shattered one by one. Then he will be receptive to the allurement of the countryside.

Children

There is nothing more relative to the subject of decentralization than children. Modern man's hyper-preoccupation with himself and his own times, and his obliviousness of his forebears and those who will come after him, is evidenced in his robbing his children of the normal rights of childhood. The modern industrial city is an externalization of adulthood. The children who are permitted existence are forced to spend their childhood within little ghettos called (laughingly enough) playgrounds. They are the prey of insistent motor cars, irrepressible industry, irate landlords and property-protecting police. Childhood, much like unemployment, is looked upon as a nuisance which receives the grudging afterthoughts of charitable institutions. The parent is reminded at every turn that his children are a nuisance to everyone. They get in the way of cars, they have no respect for "other people's" property, they overcrowd adult apartments, they cry in church, making it difficult for adults to fall into their pious semi-coma, they reduce property values—in short, they are expendable nuisances. Every block has a number of bars, a theater, a poolroom, a restaurant in which adults can recreate, but for our children there is next to nothing.

If a parent wants space for playing, a home where childhood can be permitted, a shop for repairing the damage they inevitably do, a community where children are regarded as blessings, where else can he get it but in the country? Call it escape if you will, but I prefer to look upon decentralization as the resumption of parental responsibility.

Neighborliness

One historical fact that has contributed a good deal to prejudicing people against country living is that rural life in the United States has been predominantly a Protestant phenomenon. I stress this point for its sociological significance rather than its religious implications. A people who must frequently attend church services tend to live closer together than those for whom church-going is not an essential duty. Thus the phenomenon of widely-scattered farm houses, such as was characteristic of early American rural life, would not have occurred in a Catholic country. This geographical isolation, abhorrent to human nature and intolerable among Catholics because of parochial obligations, need not be characteristic of country living, nor is it characteristic of the European countryside where rural homes nestle like so many chicks around the parish church. Yet it is geographical isolation which many people dread when they think of decentralization—an isolation neither necessary nor advisable.

On the other hand, due to factors of commerce and industry, we have achieved in our cities a geographical concentration of population so intolerable that the most likely response to a neighbor is resentment.

If I may be forgiven the paradox: apartment house dwellers are too close together to be intimate. Problems of traffic alone are so pressing as to leave little time for charitable gestures. Truly, the only way to be generous to one's city neighbor in most cases, is to get out of his way, relieve him of your presence. And that is precisely what most city neighbors do.

Properly faced, the preservation of the modern city as a social unit springs from no regard for the social nature of the individual. The divine specification that it is not proper for man to be alone cannot be applied by any stretch of the imagination, to Times Square or other city congestion. The modern city is preserved primarily because it is to the advantage of influential elements to have the support of vast numerical populations. New York City, for example, is preserved primarily because (1) it is a vast labor market, (2) it is a colossal voting block, (3) it has millions of people with money to spend right outside the shop door. All human and personal concerns have been made secondary to these numerical advantages.

Thus the city dweller is far more aware of his proximity to the folks around him as fellow workers, fellow voters and fellow shoppers, than he is to their existence as fellow neighbors. This evil cannot (in my mind) be counteracted by exhortations to neighborliness. Bear in mind the catechism lesson: you must know, love and serve God. Why must we know God? Because we cannot love anyone we do not know. The same can be applied here. One cannot love one's city neighbors because there are too many of them to know.

In the country it is possible for the individual family to know and to be known. The community of which he is part becomes intimate and comprehensible to a rural dweller in a way unexperienced by the city man. If he wishes, he can love; he can be a neighbor to the one who is in need; he can organize with others to the end of the common good; he can stand as a man among men rather than as one insignificant cog enmeshed in the city machine.

Property

It is frequently overlooked that to reconcile oneself to congested city living is to reconcile oneself to the perpetuation of mass propertylessness. To accept the industrial city is to admit that nothing can be done to see to it that men satisfy their natural right and desire for property. One need have no other urge than to own land as an incentive for moving to the country. Where else can productive property be acquired? Certainly this is no bucolic fantasy, a search for property!

For a Catholic to desire to influence social affairs implies that he must possess an area over which he has some control. If his family is now and forever beholden to a landlord, a boss, a government, subjected always to whatever secular whim may move them, in what fashion can he incarnate Christian ideas of ownership and behavior?

The lone apostle may find property an encumbrance, but the family without property will find it a vocational handicap. It will have to accept an environment over which it has no control.

Conclusion

In my experience these arguments of romance, children, neighbor and property take precedence over all matters of timeliness, composting, religious retreat or machinery. Living in the country imposes a logic within which all other matters can be measured adequately.

Decentralization is a logical step toward the rebirth of the human community, the parish and the town.